UKCAT 2014

THE IN-DEPTH GUIDE
WITH OVER 750 PRACTICE QUESTIONS
AND ANSWERS

FIRST EDITION

James Tomkins

Ordering Information:

Quantity sales. Special discounts are available on quantity purchases by corporations, associations, and others. For details, contact the publisher at the address above.

Orders by UK trade bookstores and wholesalers.

Please contact UKCATcourses: Tel: 0208 123 07 92;

Or visit www.UKCATcourses.co.uk

Printed in the United Kingdom.

All content is owned by the authors and official information regarding the test is taken from the official site www.ukcat.ac.uk and the official 2013 UKCATguide

The information within this resource is intended solely as a revision aid for the UKCAT test . Any information within the verbal reasoning sections are extracts produced by the authors and are only their opinions. The material presented is for individual private-study only; public performance of the material without written permission is specifically forbidden. All the learning resources are copyright. The views expressed are those of the authors and not those of any sponsors or partners.

Publisher's Cataloging-in-Publication data

CONTENTS

INTRODUCTION

Most students, that have reached the stage of preparation for the UKCAT, know how much work is needed in order to maximise their potential. The vision for this book is to provide the reader with an in-depth breakdown of the exam in order guide you through the most important aspects of the UKCAT. This book uses a different approach to learning aimed to provide you with the required functional skills with minimal effort.

What is in this book and how to use it effectively

This guide goes contains over 750 practice questions; including the new style questions that have been introduced to the UKCAT in 2014. The core of the book's contents, focus on understanding the concepts and skills that the UKCAT examines. The aim is to become familiar with the principles and thought-processes behind the test. Thus, it will allow for a flexible and fluid approach to virtually any question offered.

The UKCAT is a modified IQ test. Its purpose is similar to tests such as the Wechsler Adult Intelligence Scale, Wisconsin Card Sorting Test and many more. These tests provide results that medical and dental schools use as a means of assessing candidates. In order to understand the UCKAT the following breakdown, will gently touch on several important theories in neuroscience. This will help to gain an appreciation of how the brain works in each specific section, and therefore disarm some of the sections that candidates find most daunting. More importantly, knowledge of precisely what the sections are testing, will help to guide candidates in the right direction. Thus the key is to learn the system, but not to blindly memorise facts.

THE BREAKDOWN

From this point onwards you will practice your ability to learn new things and to know what the sections are testing. By the time of your exam, you will be in a position where you can effectively recall the prior information from this breakdown and know how to tackle the sections in an efficient and effective manner.

INTRODUCTION

Firstly, the concept of working memory can viewed as like a bridge, with one end of the bridge containing sensory information from your eyes, nose, ears and so on. On the other end of the bridge there are learned processes for understanding that information. They both come together to create working memory. Simply take this example:

1+5= ?

The information received from the eyes contains the shapes within the problem "1 + 5 =?" This is processed by those learned ways of understanding information to know that 1, 5 are numbers. Then in context of the other symbols it activates the skills in addition and to solve the example, 1 + 5 = 6. Thus the bridge between the two components of working memory formulates the answer 6. Most of this calculation is executed without much conscious thought or effort even. The entire exam is testing these types of bridges, but different sections connect to different learned processes of understanding information.

More detail is provided in the following sections of the book to ensure that the correct bridges to success are recognised and made more familiar. On the theme of numbers, the next chapter covers the Quantitative Reasoning (QR) section. This will provide the information needed to develop those skills and overcome any challenging problem. QR works in a similar way as the example by just activating skills that are normally covered in GCSE level mathematics.

QUANTITATIVE REASONING

Some of the key skills required for this section will be reviewed. Please note that pen and paper will be available for the test and there is a calculator provided on the screen. Use them, but use them wisely as they may use up important time.

A summary of the essential skills that will be covered is listed below, please be aware that this list is not exhaustive.

- Rounding up and down

- Unit conversions

- Reading graphs

- Calculating means, medians and mode

- Percentages & Ratios

Please note that for students that are studying A-level Maths this section may appear very simplified, but it will serve useful as a section to revise on some of the facts. When practicing these questions, try not to be too dependent on a calculator, in order to improve your mental arithmetic (and to save time in the test).

Tip - Highlight the key information in the data, understand what the question is asking and find the numbers that will give you the answer.

Rounding up and down:

Often calculations give answers to many decimal places. The answer will require rounding to the closed whole number or 1 decimal place. It is very rare to get an answer that is to two decimal places or longer. How do we round up and down efficiently?

The way to do this is if the number is five or greater you round the value up. If less than five you round it down. Imagine that a child who wants pizzas will only eat if they know their appetite will be satisfied. If there is half a pizza or more they will eat it. Anything less than half a pizza and is thrown away. The following is an example.

- If the number is **≥5 you round up**, for example 1.5 rounds up to 2
- If the number Is **<5 you round down**, for example 1.4 rounds down to 1

If the answer is like 2.3931, and you want to round it to a whole number or 1 decimal point depending in the question and answers.

For the nearest whole number, you always round the 1st decimal, 2.3931 rounds to 2. **3 is less than 5, it is less than half a pizza so you'll throw it away.** This same rule applies to round the answer to 1 decimal place, you have to round the 2nd decimal place, 2.3931 rounds to 2.4, **9 is greater than 5, is more than half a pizza so you'll take it.**

Have a go at rounding the following numbers to a whole number:

a) 21.4 rounds to ………. b) 17.8 rounds to ……….

Have a go at rounding the following numbers to 1 decimal:

c) 47.35 rounds to ………. d) 19.949 rounds to ……….

Answers

a) 21 (4 < 5)   b) 18 (8 > 5)   c) 47.4 (5 ≥ 5) d) 19.9 (4 < 5)

Tip – If a question is difficult and it is unclear whether to round up or down, just remember pizza and which slices get eaten or thrown away.

Unit conversions:

Desired Units = Units to be converted x Factor required to convert the Units

In simple terms:

Desired Units = current units x amount needed to convert

For example convert 60kg to pounds (currently in kilogram and require pounds lbs)

1kg = 2.2 lbs. In the UKCAT QR questions the factor needed to convert the units will be provided. Hence:

Desired Units (Pounds) = 60kg x 2.2

Desired Units = 132lb

132lb = 60kg

How will this be presented in the exam?

Information from the past exams shows up to 50% of your questions will be in this format with a table/graphs of data. Most questions ask to compare between different values of the data. Within the table/graph or explicitly in the question, lies the factor that is needed to convert the units. Here follows an example of this, first analyse the data to find what is required to find to the answer:

A factory has been redesigned after recent advances in technology. The old and new factories are compared in the table below. All units are per hour, unless otherwise stated. Daytime refers to the time when the factory is in production.

Category	Old factory	New factory
Daytime energy usage	20 units	23 units
Night-time energy usage	6 units	2 units
Daytime greenhouse emissions	50g	40g
Night-time greenhouse emissions	16g	10g
Power costs	£10/unit	£9/unit

What do you think is the 3 key components in this information?

1) _____

2) _____

3) _____

The 3 key components are: 1) There is an old factory. 2) There is new factory present. 3) There is data comparing the two factories in terms of energy, emissions and power costs.

The data implies allows comparison of the two factories in energy, emissions and power costs. Here is an approach to this question, using the data in the table.

In one day, if the new factory was producing for 16 hours, what was the cost of power?

- What does the question want? Cost of power. What information is available? Hours in production.
- To get to the Cost of power, first calculate the power from the hours in production and not in production.
- In the statement above the table, it states that "Daytime refers to the time when the factory is in production". In one day (24hours), 16hours is in production and 8hours not in production, which is night-time energy usage.

---

16 x 23 (Power used in production) =

8 x 2 (Power used not in production) =

Total Power used in one day=

Now convert the units of Power into cost

Your answer for Total energy used   x   Power costs =
....   x £9   =

The answer is: £3456. If this same result was not achieved, work back from the answer to look for any errors.

Percentages: Percentage is a proportion of 100.

A percentage is a proportion out of 100. This could to be shown as a decimal. This is important to remember as this provides a shortcut for most percentage based questions. Percentage can be easily converted as a proportion out of 100 or 1 which represents the whole portion. Here is how to change percentage into a decimal and how to calculate the percentage, the proportion of a given sample:

How does 87% = 0.87?

87% = 87 out of 100. This can placed in a fraction as $^{87}/_{100}$ which equals 0.87.

From a decimal you can calculate the percentage by x 100, 0.87 x 100 = 87, which is 87%

Using this principle work out a percentage from the following question.

Here is the previous table from unit conversions:

A factory has been redesigned after recent advances in technology. The old and new factories are compared in the table below. All units are per hour, unless otherwise stated. Daytime refers to the time when the factory is in production.

Category	Old factory	New factory
Daytime energy usage	20 units	23 units
Night-time energy usage	6 units	2 units
Daytime greenhouse emissions	50g	40g
Night-time greenhouse emissions	16g	10g
Power costs	£10/unit	£9/unit

What is the percentage increase in power cost per unit of the old factory compared with the new factory?

a.1% b. 9% c. 12% d. 10% e. 11%

To calculate the percentage of increase in the power cost per unit comparing the old factory to the new factory, first work out the change between the two factories.

10 - 9 = 1

Next calculate what proportion the change of power cost per unit is to the old factory

1 /10 = 0.1

Change the decimal into a percentage

0.1 x 100 = 10, which is 10%, the answer is d. 10%, the power cost per unit is 10% higher in the old factory.

An easy formula to use whenever the question asks about the percentage of the change or the difference:

The difference between the two values/The value the question want you to come it to x 100

Ratios: Ratios is comparison of proportion compared to each other

Ratios are not very different from percentages however also require the calculation of proportions. The only difference being that instead of using a value out of 100, values are calculated out of other values. Now, here is an example:

If there are six sweets in a pot, John received four sweets while Jack received two what is the proportion of sweets John received compared to Jack?

> **Firstly, the question highlights that there needs to be comparison of the proportions of John to Jack i.e John : Jack.**
>
> **Write down the values in a way that compares John : Jack. 4:2. This is the answer.**
>
> **Whenever a ratio is required, always aim to put it in the most simplified form. Both values, 4 and 2, can be divided by 2 to give you 2:1**

Now here is a UKCAT style question:

Below is a pie chart showing the burgers that 425 people chose at a fast food restaurant.

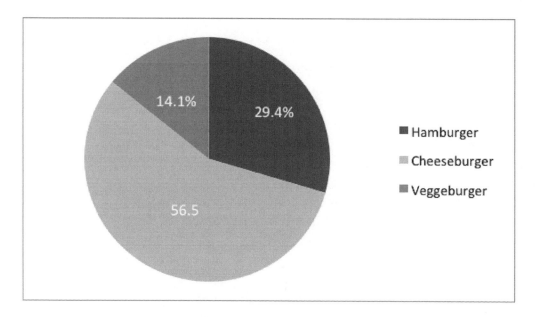

Hamburger = 29.4%, Cheeseburger = 56.5%, Veggeburger = 14.1%

Regardless of the type of question in any of the sections, aim to highlight the key components of the data and the information provided to reach the answer. In order to reinforce this, write down the two key components of the pie chart data.

The two key components are:

1) There are three different types of burgers.

2) The data is represented in a circle and the proportion out of 100 that each burger represents is also given. Now break-down a question:

What is the ratio of number of Cheeseburgers to Veggeburgers?

a.   240:60 b. 4:1 c. 12:85 d. 425:60 e. 85:12

The question asks to compare Cheeseburgers : Veggeburgers

Is the amount of Cheeseburgers : Veggeburgers known? No, therefore work out this value

What values do are known? These are the proportions out of 100, of Cheeseburgers and Veggeburgers

Hence work out the amount of Cheeseburgers and Veggeburgers

Cheeseburgers:

56.5% proportion of 425 = 425 x 0.565 which equals 240.125. This rounds down to 240.

Veggeburgers:

14.1% proportion of 425 = 425 x 0.141 which equals 59.925. This rounds up to 60.

So now know the ratio is 240:60

Aim to put it to the values in the simplest form. 240 and 60 can be divided by 60 to give you 4:1

The answer is b. 4:1

Reading graphs

There is a wide range of graphs that could be used in the UKCAT. Most graphs only require data extraction to derive a value from it. The way to read from a bar graph will not be covered here (this can be found in GCSE Maths textbooks). Therefore the focus is on the most common example: pie charts.

In the example below, the approach to a pie chart question will be demonstrated.

The previous data from will be used to focus on the question rather than analysing the data. Firstly, a key thing to understand is that a pie chart is the representation of data in a form of a circle, a whole circle = 360o

Below is a pie chart showing which shows types of burgers 425 people chose at a fast food restaurant.

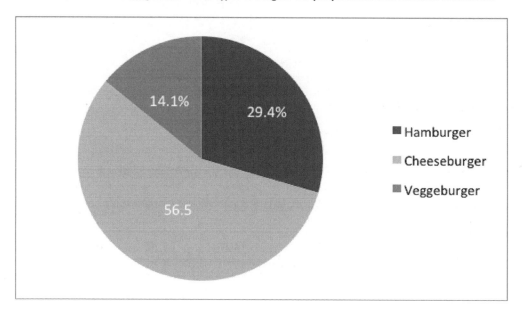

Hamburger = 29.4%, Cheeseburger = 56.5%, Veggeburger = 14.1%

What angle does the Cheeseburger section take up on the pie chart? Give answer to the closest whole angle

a.   57 b. 203 c. 204 d. 202 e. 56

Going back to two key components, what data is known? This is the proportion out of 100% that Cheeseburgers represent. Remember that a full circle, 100%, = 360o.

Here is how to calculate the answer:

Calculating mean, median and mode

What is the mean? Mean is often used interchangeably with the word average. It is the sum of the values divided by the number of values. The aim is to find out the value represents all of the data.

$$\text{The mean} = \frac{\text{Sum of the data}}{\text{the amount of data}}$$

What is the median? This is the value at the middle of the data. This is most easily calculated by first rearranging all the data in order of size. Then, in order to find the middle value, calculate the total number of values. After this, add one to the total number of values and divide this new number by two. For an even total number of values a non whole number is derived. To make this clear, layout four coins, or any four objects that are easily available in a line. Place a finger on the middle point of the objects. This is in between the second and the third object, (hence 2.5). Therefore, this is the same as adding the two values that the midpoint is in between and then, dividing that number by 2.

$$\text{The median} = \frac{\text{the amount of data} + 1}{2}$$

Mode is the more straightforward concept. Simply, it is the most common data: the number that appears most frequently.

Now, here is a UKCAT style question:

Below is a stem and leaf plot showing the average scores of people that took the UKCAT test on a specific day at a test centre. The left column represents hundreds, the right represents tens.

```
4    8 9
5    0 1 2 3 3 6 8 8 8
6    2 3 4 5 5 5 5
7    0 1 2 3 3 8
8    1 3
```

What do you think are the 2 key components in this plot?

1) _____

2) _____

The two key components in this plot are: 1) The left column represents hundreds and the right column represents tens 2) The data is already ordered in value.

Now work out the following:

What is the modal score?

a. 630 b. 580 c. 650 d. 650 e. 580

What is the median score?

a. 650 h. 645 c. 630 d. 635 e. 640

What is the mean score?

a. 600 b. 619 c. 640 d. 629 e. 630

The data is arranged in ascending order value, which speeds up the process of working out the mean, median and mode.

1) What is the modal score? c. 650 - is the score that occurs the most.

2) What is the median score?

$$\textbf{The median} = {}^{\textbf{the amount of data +1}}/_{\textbf{2}}$$

The total number of students is 26, so the midpoint would be the 13.5th score, to work this out, add the 13th and the 14th value, 630 + 640 = 1270. Now divide this number by 2. 1270 ÷ 2 = 635, the answer is d. 635.

1) What is the mean score?

$$\textbf{The mean} = {}^{\textbf{Sum of the data}}/_{\textbf{the amount of data}}$$

480 + 490 + 500 + 510 + 520 + 530 + 530 + 560 + 580 + 580 + 580 + 620 +630 + 640 + 650 + 650 + 650 +650 + 700 + 710 + 720 + 730 + 730 + 780 + 810 + 830 = 16,360. Mean is 16,360/26 = 629.23, so 629

d. 629

The aim is to be able to perform all of these skills without even having to think about it. This will be achieved by understanding the concepts. Practice UKCAT questions is a valuable resource, but, an even better resources to master theses skills can be found in real life. Open up a pack of Haribos, and calculate the ratio of, for example, gummy rings to cola bottles to other sweets. Convert the units: If the ratio is 3 : 5 : 2 and the packet costs £1.00, what is the cost of each type of sweet? £1.00 ÷ 10 gives the total number i.e the sum of the ratios. One sweet in the ratio is worth 10p and so five cola bottles is worth 50p of the packet. What is the percentage increase of cola bottles to gummy rings? This will not only help to understand the skills but it will also improve mental arithmetic and reduce dependence on a calculator. As the precise content of the questions that will come up in the exam is unknown, by practising this it will build the right bridges and help to maintain a relaxed, flexible and adaptable approach to the questions. These are the key skills in achieving the best in this section.

Content the past exams suggest that the other 50% of questions will be in a statement format. The values that needed to answer the question will not be presented obviously in a table or graph. It requires the ability to read the statement and pick out key information from it. Instead of giving an example of a statement, the next section containing the breakdown of Decision Analysis and Verbal Reasoning will also help you tackle these types of statement-based questions.

DECISION ANALYSIS

Before the breakdown of this section, remember, do not attempt to memorise any of the neuroscience. It will not help in the exam.

The understanding of words is more complicated then calculations. However, this is something that is done on a constant basis, even right now. The information from this sentence is being processed into the shapes to one side of the bridge, similar to the numbers. On the other side of this bridge, the shapes are converted to letters. The letters, then go on and become the information side of another bridge. The letters then either 1) go directly to a mental library of words and related information or 2) Take a detour. They are translated to sounds, just like how you a child would sound out letters when first learning words. The destination of the words is the mental library.

In the mental library, the meaning of the word is recognised, and used to trigger related information like how it is combined in sentences and what words have similar meanings. Just like the genres that are found in a library. A sequence of words is put into context by the brain in an order that makes the best sense. Now here is an example of how all of this works:

The pupils rose to the teacher.

Rose has two meaning 1) the past tense form of the verb to rise and 2) a flower.

To break this down, there are Recognised shapes → Transformed into letters → Converted letters to words → Words are then processed in the mental library → Which then, chooses the best form of "rose" that suits the context and presented an interpretation of the meaning of the sentence. This happens all in the space of milliseconds. That is how powerful the brain is at processing verbal information. It is this processing that is tested in the Decision Analysis and Verbal Reasoning sections of the UKCAT. The process of how to use this mental library is the main focus. Now here are more example questions that allow the practice of these processes.

Useful classification of words

Class	General meaning	Easy way to classify it
Noun	A thing	Any word you can place, the- in front of
Adjective	Modifies nouns	Any word you can place is- or I'm- in front of it
Verbs	Usually signifies action	Any word you can place to- in front

D= cold, 6= apple, 7=grapes

D(6,7) = ?

Cold is an adjective, so it needs a noun from the combination of (6,7) to modify and make sense.

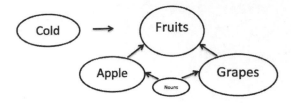

D(6,7) = Cold fruits

Now, try two harder questions that are more like what will come up in the exam:

A = Several	1 = Animal	! = White
B = Only	2 = Vegetable	@ = Green
C = Eat	3 = Plant	£ = Like
D = Drink	4 = Fruit	$ = Black
E = Use	5 = Fire	% = Hot
F = Future	6 = Water	^ = Cold
G = Before	7 = Smoke	& = Wet
H = Other	8 = Steam	
J = Lots	9 = Tree	
K = Male	10 = Sky	
L = Reverse	11 = Cloud	
M = Grow	12 = Sand	
H = Generalise	13 = Soil	
	14 = Cow	
	15 = Baby	
	16 = Adult	

1) What is the best interpretation of the following coded message? (13, &), M, 3

   Plants will grow when it rains

   Plants will grow from wet soil

   Wet plants will grow from the soil

   Vegetation will grow from the soil

   The wet soil will result in vegetation

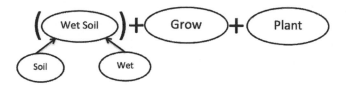

Combination of the noun – Soil, and the adjective –Wet, leads to what phrase? – Wet Soil

The correct answer is Plants will grow from wet soil

Why are the other options not the best interpretation?

Plants will grow when It rains – No mention of soil

Wet plants will grow from the soil – Incorrect order of words, (13,&), Soil and wet are combined

Vegetation will grow from the soil - No mention of wet

The wet soil will result in vegetation – This is a related combination of the words but a simpler and better interpretation of the original words exists. This would be the best interpretation of the code out of the wrong answers.

The other 50% of your questions will be split between two formats. One requires the coding of a sentence and the other is to highlight two words that would provide a better interpretation of the sentence. The latter is easy to do and will be covered in the practice questions section of Decision Analysis.

2) What would the best way to encode the following message be? The man ate smoked beef

(16,K), C(L, F), (7, 14)

16, C(L, F), (7, 14)

K, C(L, F), (7, 14)

(16,K), C, (8, 14)

(16,K), C(L, F), (8, 14)

Key tip – For this format of question, work against the natural flow of Verbal processing. Aim to choose between the two or more options, by placing the combinations together to find the answers, which "feels" the best and most accurate. Remember this is an innate process developed from a young age, thus can be used to gain an advantage.

Here breakdown this sentence below, aim to use the mental store to explore the meaning of the words contributing to this sentence, limited to the coded words above, form a close representation of the sentence:

The man ate smoked beef

The man – A noun, of an adult male.

Ate – Past tense form of the verb to eat.

smoked beef – the noun beef, combined with an verb smoked.

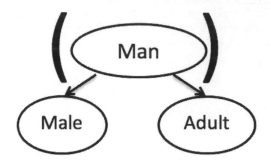

The man – (16, K)

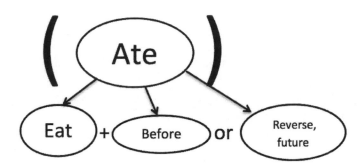

Eat – C, Past can be represented as either before, G or reverse of future (L,F). (L,F) is more accurate to the past tense and is the best way to encode past tense as an individual word. Ate is – C(L,F). Here is an opportunity to use the natural flow of verbal processing to check the answer is correct. Which of the two available options, before eat, or reverse future eat, "feels" like the best interpretation of ate?

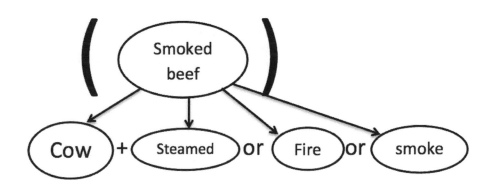

Smoked beef – Closest noun to beef is Cow (14), smoked can be represented as either steamed (8), fire (5) or smoke

(7). Remember the aim is to find the most accurate way to represent smoked. The best way to encode smoked as an individual word, would be to take the present form of the verb, smoke (7). Smoked beef is - (7,14). Here is another great opportunity to use the natural flow of Verbal processing to check the answer. Which of the three available options: steamed cow; fire cow or smoke cow, "feels" like the best interpretation of smoked beef?

The correct answer to The man ate smoked beef is (16,K), C(L,F), (7,14)

Why?

16, (L, F)C, (7, 14) – Adult ate smoke cow - Adult could be either male or female.

 K, (L, F)C, (7, 14) – Male ate smoke cow - Male could be either boy or man.

(16,K), C, (8, 14) – Man eat steamed cow - eat is in the present tense, steamed is not the most accurate form of smoked.

(16,K), (L, F)C, (8, 14) – Man ate steamed cow - steamed is not the most accurate form of smoked.

Key takeaway point – The best resource to use for these questions the mind! There is mental store containing an abundance of words with meaning, context and associations. Use it and trust instinct.

Next, is an in-depth explanation of Verbal Reasoning. Take a moment to let the skills previously learned settle in.

Before moving on to the practice questions of the Decision Analysis section, appreciate the breakdown and use those questions to develop understanding.

VERBAL REASONING

Now that how the brain sees and processes verbal information has been covered.

What is the Verbal Reasoning section testing? – It is testing the ability to analyse and criticise verbal information presented in a passage. It combines the verbal processing of decision analysis and the ability to read the passage and highlight key information that will achieve the right answer, like in the QR section.

Here is a practice passage, which is part of an interactive breakdown. Get involved, circle the answers that are correct and write down the answer in the spaces provided. Any mistakes made are the best resource in order to develop and improve.

Below is an extract from an article on the Food Industry:

Traditional restaurants present their diners with a regimented menu; meanwhile diners themselves are becoming more concerned as to the exact contents of their meals, particularly given the high media interest in health and nutrition.

"How many times have we left plates of unfinished food at the end of a meal? Or left having felt hungry? Have you ever really wanted to order a particular dish, but didn't because it came with mushrooms, but you wanted something else? We all have different dietary requirements and desires – the time has come for this to be reflected in restaurant menus. Yes, a printed menu usually has a variety of options, but these menus fail to cater to differences in size of appetite, health-consciousness, allergies and intolerances, all at the same time!"

The problem we have identified is that customers wanting to express themselves in the above ways are required to over-come many obstacles to achieve this goal. From the hassle of embarrassing conversations with waiters, who then communicate this to the kitchen, to the hope that the final plate will account for the requested changes.

We aim to solve this by allowing our customers' exact requirements to be communicated directly to the kitchen using the ingenious interface of an iPad app. Not only does this allow for an engaging, novelty experience, but it also serves an important purpose in cutting out the unnecessary steps in getting what the customer wants.

"From 2013 onwards, restaurants will need to make customisation a cornerstone of their food"

-       Technomic Inc., the food industry's leading research analyst.

Questions

1)   The passage was written by Technomic Inc.

True   False   Can't Tell

2)   The passage was probably not written by Technomic Inc.

True   False   Can't Tell

3)   The first quote was from Technomic Inc.

True   False   Can't Tell

4)   The first quote may be from Technomic Inc.

True   False   Can't Tell

5)   The passage states that restaurants generally have strict menus.

True   False   Can't Tell

6)   Customers who do not wish to customise their meal tend to have an easier time ordering than those that do.

True   False   Can't Tell

7)   Customers will have to bring their iPad to order at this restaurant.

True   False   Can't Tell

8)   Customers will require an iPad to order at this restaurant.

True   False   Can't Tell

9)   According to the text, waiters embarrass customers.

True   False   Can't Tell

10)   The text suggests that-

a)   Customers are often embarrassed when talking to waiters about altering a meal on the menu;

b)   iPads are the best way to offer customisation to customers in restaurants

c)   When customers request changes, the final plate often does not include these

d)   Vegetarians have hard times in restaurants.

How to process the passage

Each paragraph of a passage is written with a certain objective. Skim read the passage, and highlight the objective of that paragraph. This allows the quick and efficient location of the answer to the question. Do not attempt to memorise the passage as visual information decays quickly and the concise meaning of the passage is lost.

Now here an example of how to breakdown the passage into this format:

Below is an extract from an article on the Food Industry:

"Traditional restaurants present their diners with a regimented menu; meanwhile diners themselves are becoming more concerned as to the exact contents of their meals, particularly given the high media interest in health and nutrition."

Current ways of doing things and changes in the demand of restaurants

"How many times have we left plates of unfinished food at the end of a meal? Or left having felt hungry? Have you ever really wanted to order a particular dish, but didn't because it came with mushrooms, but you wanted something else? We all have different dietary requirements and desires – the time has come for this to be reflected in restaurant menus. Yes, a printed menu usually has a variety of options, but these menus fail to cater to differences in size of appetite, health-consciousness, allergies and intolerances, all at the same time!"

A quote highlighting, negative customers experience when ordering a customised meal

"The problem we have identified is that customers wanting to express themselves in the above ways are required to over-come many obstacles to achieve this goal. From the hassle of embarrassing conversations with waiters, who then communicate this to the kitchen, to the hope that the final plate will account for the requested changes."

Current problems in the process of ordering a customised meal

"We aim to solve this by allowing our customers' exact requirements to be communicated directly to the kitchen using the ingenious interface of an iPad app. Not only does this allow for an engaging, novelty experience, but it also serves an important purpose in cutting out the unnecessary steps in getting what the customer wants."

Solution to the problems of ordering a meal, how to supply the demand of the customer

"From 2013 onwards, restaurants will need to make customisation a cornerstone of their food"

-       Technomic Inc., the food industry's leading research analyst.

Concluding quote

How to process the questions

The questions are notoriously difficult in this section. Here the question is going to be broken down into two key components:

1.   Where to look for the answer

2.   What is the question asking?

1)   The passage was written by Technomic Inc.

Where to look for the required information: The passage – The whole passage is referred to.

What information is the question specifically interested in: Written by Technomic Inc - identify the author, is it Technomic Inc?

2) The passage was probably not written by Technomic Inc.

Where to look for the required information: The passage – The whole passage is referred to.

What information is the question specifically interested in: Probably not written by – The author is not Technomic Inc

3) The first quote was from Technomic Inc.

Where to look for the required information: The first quote of the passage (A quote highlighting, negative customers experience when ordering a customised meal)

What information is the question specifically interested in: The author is Technomic Inc

4) The first quote may be from Technomic Inc.

Where to look for the required information: The first quote of the passage (A quote highlighting, negative customers experience when ordering a customised meal)

What information is the question specifically interested in: may be from Technomic Inc. – could the author be Technomic Inc.?

5) The passage states that restaurants generally have strict menus.

Where to look for the required information: Although the words "The passage" may lead you to think the location is within the entire passage, the latter "restaurants generally have strict menus" leads to the section - Current ways of doing things and changes in the demand of restaurants.

What information is the question specifically interested in: do restaurants generally have strict menus?

6) Customers who do not wish to customise their meal tend to have an easier time ordering than those that do.

Where to look for the required information: The comparison of the experience of ordering food - A quote highlighting, negative customers experience when ordering a customised meal

What information is the question specifically interested in: Comparison of the experience of customers who want to order food without customising it Vs those who do. Customers who don't customise their meal have an easier time ordering than those who do. The question can also be rephrased as Customers who customise their meal have a harder time ordering than those who don't.

7)   Customers will have to bring their iPad to order at this restaurant.

Where to look for the required information: an iPad app is offered as solution to the problem so any information about the iPads will be in the section - Solution to the problems of ordering a meal, how to supply the demand of the customer

What information is the question specifically interested in: Is there any clear indications that a customer will have to use their own iPad?

8)   Customers will require an iPad to order at this restaurant.

Where to look for the required information: Same as above

What information is the question specifically interested in: Is there any clear indication that a customer will have to use an iPad to order at this restaurant

9)   According to the text, waiters embarrass customers.

Where to look for the required information: "The text" is misleading. The word waiter would be mentioned in either the experience or problems of ordering a customised meal

What information is the question specifically interested in: Do the waiters embarrass the customers?

11)   The text suggests that-

In this format of questions, there is a leading statement and the challenge is to choose one of the four options presented that suits the statement. The statement holds the key to what information is required. Out of the four options, the statement looks for either, what statement is TRUE or what is FALSE. Be careful reading the statement. It is often asked in an over complicated manor.

What information is this statement interested in? The text suggests that or, in simple terms, which of the following statements is true.

a)   Customers are often embarrassed when talking to waiters about altering a meal on the menu;

Where to look for the required information: as mentioned in the explanation of 9) either the experience or problems of ordering a customised meal

24

b)   iPads are the best way to offer customisation to customers in restaurants

Where to look for the required information: iPads, indicates the section - Solution to the problems of ordering a meal, how to supply the demand of the customer.

c)   When customers request changes, the final plate often does not include this.

Where to look for the required information: key focus is communication that is looked upon in the section - Current problems in the process of ordering a customised meal.

d)   Vegetarians have hard times in restaurants.

Where to look for the required information: key focus is experience, so the section - A quote highlighting, negative customers experience when ordering a customised meal.

Remember, the leading statement aims to either find the TRUE option among the FALSE/ CAN'T TELL options, or the FALSE/ CAN'T TELL option among the TRUE options. For this example the leading statement aims to find the TRUE option among the FALSE/ CAN'T TELL options.

Answers

1.   Can't Tell. The final quote has been attributed to Technomic Inc., but there is no author given for the whole passage.

2.   True. If the passage had been written by Technomic Inc., it probably would not have specified where the final quote came from. The word "probably" is aimed to create ambiguity with the answer. A common pitfalls students make is focusing on this ambiguity and chose can't tell

3.   Can't Tell. The first quote of passage is the entire second paragraph. The author has not stated the source of the quote, so this may or may not be true. With any doubt the answer is can't tell.

4.   True. As there is no one credited to the first quote, this is a possibility. Key word in this question is "may be", stating ambiguity. A simplified form of this question is – Is there any ambiguity about the author of the 1st quote?

5.   False The passage states this is for traditional restaurants, not restaurants in general. "Traditional restaurants present their diners with a regimented menu"

6.   True. "Identified is that customers wanting to express themselves in the above ways are required to overcome many obstacles to achieve this goal" so compare the two diners who want the same meal. The text suggests that, customers who wish to change the meal in the menu have to overcome obstacles. And therefore have a harder time ordering the same meal.

7.   Can't Tell. "ingenious interface of an iPad app" The passage does not state whether customers would have to bring their own iPad, or whether the restaurant would provide them with one.

8.   True. The passage says that an iPad app will be used, so it can assumed an iPad will be needed.

9.   False. "From the hassle of embarrassing conversations with waiters" A common pitfall students make, is because visual information decays rapidly over time. The brain remembers the sentence as, customers + embarrassing + waiters. When it comes to processing a sentence, it is faster to recognise words in a sentence that do not make sense but are grammatically correct. Under exam pressure and in a state of anxiety, students recognise the key words, customers + embarrassing + waiters and the fact they are grammatically correct. However, failing to recognise the real meaning of the question. The way to avoid this trap is, to read over the abstract and question concisely and consistently for each question. Do not choose an answer until both the question and the area it focuses on are fully understand.

10. The text suggests that-

a)   Customers are often embarrassed when talking to waiters about altering a meal on the menu. The passage states that customers have embarrassing conversations with waiters. "From the hassle of embarrassing conversations with waiters." Therefore this option is TRUE

Why are the others False/Can't tell?

b)   iPads are the best way to offer customisation to customers in restaurants

"The ingenious interface of an iPad app. Not only does this allow for an engaging, novelty experience, but it also serves as an important purpose in cutting out the unnecessary steps in getting what the customer wants" – There is no reference to how effective it is, or whether it is the best way. Therefore this option is CAN'T TELL

c)   When customers request changes, the final plate often does not include these

The quote - "to the hope that the final plate will account for the requested changes" is about the uncertainty of whether the final plate will have the changes included. There is no specific information such as figures to show the final plate does not include the changes. Therefore this option is FALSE

d)   Vegetarians have hard times in restaurants.

There is no reference to vegetarians in the passage so, this mean their experiences in restaurants are not known. Therefore this option is CAN'T TELL

.Key takeaway points –

-       Avoid the common pitfall of rushing to an answer.

-       Make sure the breakdown of the passage helps to locate where the required information for the questions can be found.

- Breakdown each question to create a concise meaning of the question

- Reread the passage for each question – visual information decays quickly. The interpretation of what has been read has to be refreshed for each question.

- Do not compensate with existing knowledge. If it is not in the text having looked through the entire passage, it is likely to be either a False/Can't Tell answer.

Again, UKCAT questions is a valuable resource. But try to master theses skills in real life! Next time a passage is available to read, whether it is from a newspaper or online, break it down and highlight the key objective of each paragraph. While you doing this, also practice Decision Analysis by highlighting a word and thinking what two other words can combine to make that word

Understanding is the key. As the content of the questions that come up in the test are unknown, it allows building of the right bridges and connections to virtually handle any question that can come up.

Next, a thorough an in-depth explanation of Abstract Reasoning follows below. This section is quite tricky. Again, a break is recommended at this point.

Before the practice questions of the Decision Analysis and Verbal Reasoning sections, reread the breakdown in order to have a good understanding of what the test sections require.

ABSTRACT REASONING

So far, a basic understanding of the principals of problem solving in the UKCAT exam has been gained. Abstract reasoning is not all that different from other sections. The focus of this section is the analysis of shapes and being able to recognise patterns within them. The mind processes visual information in two ways simultaneously: what and where. One important pitfall to avoid is changing the shapes into symbols, giving them meaning from prior memory. For example, often, when looking at an arrow shape it is easy to spend too much time trying to look for a connection to do with direction. The way to avoid this is to remember that the shapes are in abstract. They hold no greater meaning then just a shape.

Before the breakdown of this section, have a pen handy. It will be required to draw in a box. This is key because it will help to develop the skills tested in this section. It is recommend that a pen is used because any mistakes will provide vital insight to the thought process involved, and highlight areas that are not understand clearly. It will show how to improve the skills in this section.

Key aspects to look at:

- Symbol

- Size

- Quantities

- Colour

- Symmetry

- Direction

- Positioning

- Angles

- Multiple Rules

This is a long list, however it is unnecessary and to consuming to try to remember this entire list . It would also be ineffective because under exam pressure there is an increased likelihood that it will be difficult to recall all the cold facts like this. Fortunately, many of these aspects like Symbol, Size, Colour, can be observed and processed without having to put much thought into it. A good way to progress is to use mistakes as learning tools. Try to remember sections forgotten and missed out and make sure this is not repeated. As the questions progress, if it is difficult to find a pattern, try starting again in a effort to look at the aspects that can be found naturally.

Information from the past exams, suggest that 90% of your answers will be in the format of: "what set does this box fall into" - A, B or neither. The other 10% of the answers will be in the format of "what box completes the series." Provided is an in-depth breakdown of each format because the way to tackle these formats are different. A good starting point for both formats is to think - what is the pattern in the Set/Steps of the series?

Now, go through this sample question: For the following questions see if the box falls into either: Set A, Set B or Neither. In the designated spaces, write down what the pattern could be.

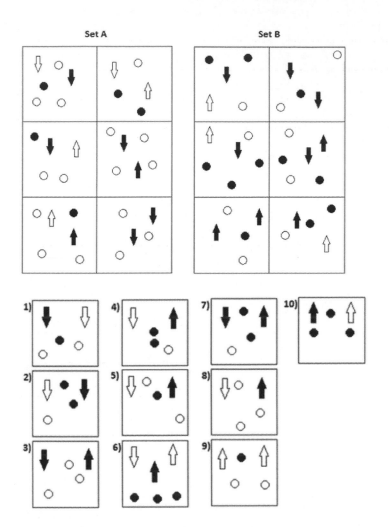

What do you think is the key information and information you can eliminate in order to find the pattern?

_____

_____

_____

_____

_____

_____

_____

_____

_____

_____

As stated previously, a common pitfall that applicants make is focusing solely on trying to recognise patterns that are not there. The purpose of the shapes is to be overwhelming and intimidating. Once a shape is recognised, the mind naturally processes this as a symbol looking for meaning and patterns. In this example the arrow shape is being process, which is a symbol that indicates direction. Most students are drawn to look for directions and changes regarding the direction. This is an attempt to distract from the real, simple pattern. From the Sets direction of the arrow can be discarded because it inconsistently points in different direction. In order to understand this process of eliminating unnecessary shapes, the question above is use but the arrows have been replaced with circles.

What could the pattern be?

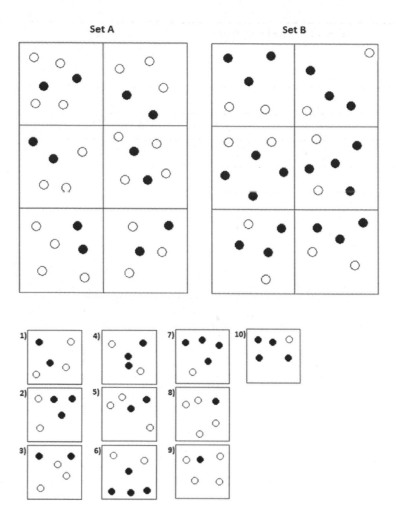

Now, the arrow has been eliminated, the pattern is a lot easier to recognise.

A key point to take away from this is do not become preoccupied with what the shape means in real life and try to look for an overcomplicated complicated pattern. The shapes are in abstract; they do not represent anything else but a shape.

Rule: Set A has two black shapes, Set B has two white shapes.

Answers

1) A

2) B

3) A

4) B

5) A

6) B

7) Neither

8) Neither

9) Neither

10) Neither

Attempt the following example, what can be seen?

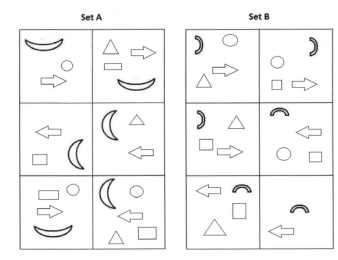

What do you think is the key information and information you can eliminate in order to find the pattern?

_____

_____

_____

_____

_____

_____

_____

_____

_____

_____

_____

Firstly, what is consistent? Both sets contain triangles, ovals, quadrilaterals and a crescent shape. There is not a clear indication of a change in size, colour or quantities in the Sets. There seems to be no clear pattern in the amount of shapes, type of shapes or even position of the shapes for either A or B as there are some boxes without triangles, ovals etc. One thing that is noticed is the change in the crescent shape in A and B. Also one shape, which is consistent in the boxes of A and B, is the arrow. So now simplify the example and try to notice the pattern now.

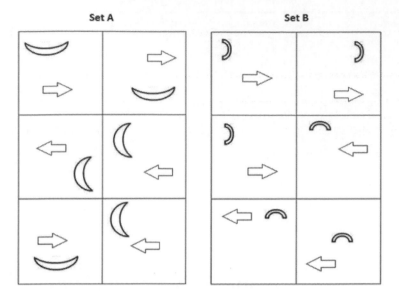

What seems to be changing? Firstly specify

⇧ = 0º

The arrows are rotated to either, 90º or 270º.

 The plane of the crescent shape also changes, from on a vertical or horizontal axis. Is there a connection between the two shapes? Simplified further:

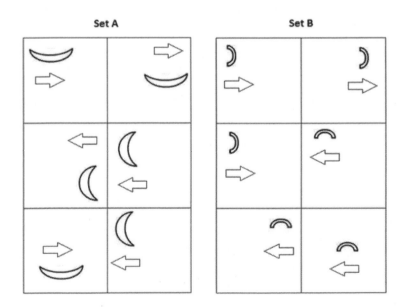

In Set A, if arrow is at 90o, the crescent shape is on the Horizontal axis, if at 270o, the crescent shape is on the Vertical axis

In Set B, if arrow is a 90o, the crescent shape is on the Vertical axis, if at 270o, the crescent shape is on the Horizontal axis
Or vice versa if the crescent shape is on the Horizontal axis, the arrow is a 90o

Admittedly, although it would have been easier to state the arrow as left or right, that would change the arrow shape into a symbol. The arrow can be replaced with any symbol that has one line of symmetrical such as:

Which Set does this box fall into, A, B or neither?

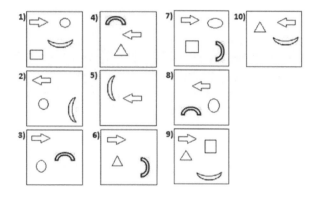

Answers

1) A

2) A

3) Neither

4) B

5) A

6) B

7) B

8) B

9) A

10) Neither

If any of the answers achieved have been wrong thus fare, regardless of if it seems clear now, it is STRONGLY recommend that reread from the beginning of this section to firmly understand the concepts.

Have a go at this example.

Set A

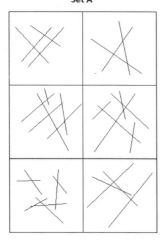

Set B

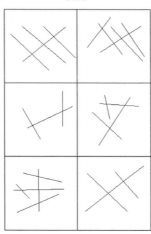

What do you think is the key information and information you can eliminate in order to find the pattern?
_____
_____
_____
_____

The mind processes visual information as what and where. In context of this question, what is simple, there are just Lines. There is not any other shape involved in the question. That eliminates the concerns about colour and shading. The length of the lines vary within both sets of data so that can be eliminated. The quantity of the lines are also varied so this can be eliminated that. What can be eliminated from possible factors that make up the pattern? This could include the positioning, angles and symmetry and so on.

This leaves the key question, where is the pattern in these Sets? To overcome the intimidating lines and make them easier to process, they will be simplified using the information stated above. Here the edges have been trimmed off the lines. Focus on where the pattern lies

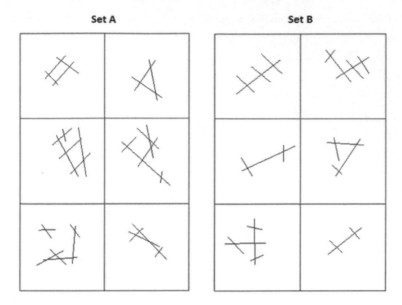

Set A

Set B

What can the pattern be? Is it the amount of lines that cross one specific line?

Set A has one enclosed space. Set B has no enclosed spaces. This might be harder to see in the box of the second column of the third row in Set A:

Set A

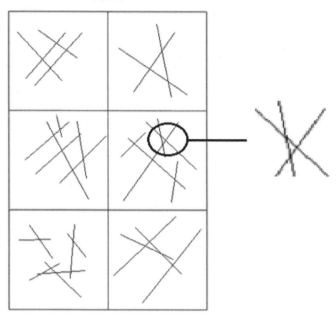

Here are the accompanying questions to gain a familiarity with this format. Where to boxes fall? Choose between: Set A, Set B or Neither

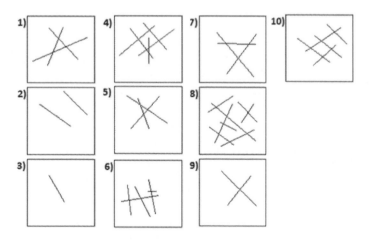

Answers

1) A

2) B

3) B

4) A

5) A

6) B

7) A

8) A

9) B

10) A

Here is the second format of questions. It requires all the skills of decoding and recognising and eliminating information stated through above. The question will be laid out like this: four steps will be provided that are changing in sequence, the question will then ask to pick the fifth step in the series.

The breakdown of this example follows and will provide a guide through the process. Please draw in the designated boxes in the following example, grab a pen and pick up on your mistakes.

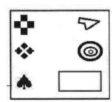 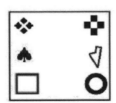

Draw what you think is the next box in this series

What is consistent? There are 6 distinguishable shapes. Three lines on each vertical border of the box.

Going from the 1st step to the 2nd, what stays the same? The shapes:

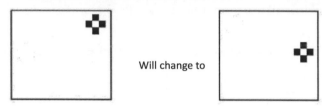 do not change. The shape 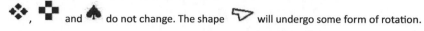 will undergo some form of rotation.

There are still 6 distinguishable shapes. Three lines are on each vertical border of the box. So presume the three shapes will stay the space in the following step. What has changed? All the shapes seem to have moved one position in a clock wise direction, so presume that:

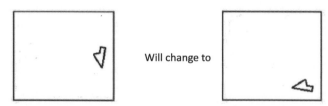

Will change to

The shape 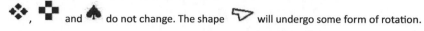 has rotated at 90°, so we can presume:

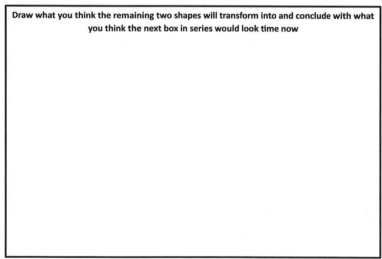

Will change to

Now having gained an understanding of what is happening and what to look for, what will the remaining two shapes will transform into?

> **Draw what you think the remaining two shapes will transform into and conclude with what you think the next box in series would look time now**

The answer

43

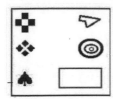  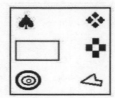

Did the box drawn match up to the answer? If not, try and build up on the pattern assumed from Step 1-2 to Step 2-3. Eliminate any incorrect patterns and analyse the ones that fit.

Hopefully insight has been gained about the information required, and how to process the information in a way that will give an accurate pattern. To reinforce the process of looking at previous step to get your pattern, draw the box for the fourth box in the series, using steps 2-3.

Draw what you think is the next box in this series

The answer

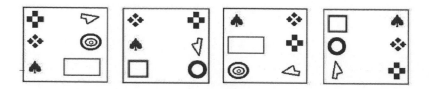

This example was broken down to help provide a guide through the process needed to get to the right pattern. Now, here is how how this type of question will come up in the UKCAT, with a small change to the layout.

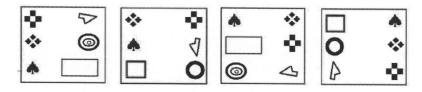

From the following options, which figure completes the series?

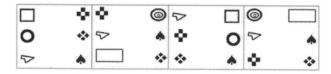

Draw your answer here

45

The answer is:

Key takeaway points-

• These are shapes NOT symbols

• What is consistent in the data? Aim to eliminate useless shapes that are placed to overwhelm and distract, focus on the shapes that will help to lead to a correct pattern.

• Breakdown each shape, analyse what it does. Is it useful or useless? Does it change? If so find out a reason why.

Take a break , or even better a quick nap. Let the skills you have just learnt settle in, refresh your mind. So you are fully prepared to understand the next section.

SITUATIONAL JUDGMENT TEST

This section is a more straightforward part of the exam. It is a personality test that is ethically and patient based. Patients place a significant amount of trust in medical professionals to take care of their health. This applies in many different settings such as in a hospital, or a dental surgery or even the opticians. What qualities are expected of the healthcare practitioner who oversees patient care? The aim of the Situational Judgment Test is to assess whether candidates display these qualities. Now the key qualities that are expected from medical professionals will be broken down, will provide a good framework to handle these questions but it is not an exhaustive list:

Main priority is the care of the patient, this means it is important to display:

- Trust.

- Integrity.

This expands to an umbrella of key ethical aspects:

- Being polite and considerate – Respect the patient.

- Be a good listener; understand the patients concerns and preference in general but more importantly in regards to their care and treatment.

- Patient confidentiality.

This is essential because candidates are in a position of responsibility this means:

- Be prepared to explain your actions.

- Prepare to act quickly if the patient is going to be compromised in terms of safety, or any other aspect such as comfort or dignity.

- Be responsible for your knowledge and skills; and understand limitations in that knowledge.

- Co-ordinate with others in ways, which are in best interest of the patient.

- Judgment of capacity and consent.

In summary, the key is to display a respect for human life. These are all of qualities expected from a medical professional overseeing patient care.

Now work through an example of a scenario and choose the most appropriate the action to take in the scenario:

A drug addict visits her GP. She says she is finding her treatment tough, and has relapsed once. She has a young son. Social services previously found her fit to look after him, but this was before the relapse. She says she finds it tough to look after him at the moment. How appropriate are each of the following responses.

Now examine this situation, like the Verbal reasoning analyse the situation, write down key aspects of patient care that are being tested.

Write down the key aspects of patient care that you think the situation wants you to look at
_____
_____
_____
_____
_____
_____
_____
_____
_____
_____
_____

A drug addict visits her GP. – The patient is a drug addict; a key area to start thinking about is the capacity to make decisions. Are the decisions made in the best interest of the patient? Responsibility of the health of the patient both physically and psychologically lies with the GP. She says she is finding her treatment tough, and has relapsed once. – Again the patient's care needs to be addressed by the GP, who will need to listen to the patient's concerns regarding her treatment and management. Why is she finding it difficult? Is there an alternative treatment? She has a young son. Social services previously found her fit to look after him, but this was before the relapse. She says she finds it tough to look after him at the moment. – Here is the moral dilemma, faced with the conflicting situation of patient confidentiality versus the care of her son. Key points to remember, healthcare professionals are meant to be trustworthy and act with integrity. The patient's care is the primary concern not the care of the son. How appropriate are each of the following responses.

Circle the answer that is most correct.

1) Although consent should be sought, if the child's safety is at risk, there is a case to call social services anyway -

a) A very appropriate thing to do

b) Appropriate, but not ideal

c) Inappropriate, but not awful

d) A very inappropriate thing to do

2) This allows for the patient to consent. The doctor should support the patient at all times

a) A very appropriate thing to do

b) Appropriate, but not ideal

c) Inappropriate, but not awful

d) A very inappropriate thing to do

3) If the child's safety is at risk, there is a case to call social services without consent

a) A very appropriate thing to do

b) Appropriate, but not ideal

c) Inappropriate, but not awful

d) A very inappropriate thing to do

4) This would help the patient get back on track –

a) A very appropriate thing to do

b) Appropriate, but not ideal

c) Inappropriate, but not awful

d) A very inappropriate thing to do

5) Determine whether the child is at risk, but may take a while –

a) A very appropriate thing to do

b) Appropriate, but not ideal

c) Inappropriate, but not awful

d) A very inappropriate thing to do

The model answers

1) Although consent should be sought, if the child's safety is at risk, there is a case to call social services anyway - Appropriate, but not ideal. Here there is a good case doing so and this action can be justified. However, if the patient does not consent it violates patient confidentiality and trust.

2) This allows for the patient to consent. The doctor should support the patient at all times. A very appropriate thing to do – The patient is the key priority and the main focus of care should be with her.

3) If the child's safety is at risk, there is a case to call social services without consent Inappropriate, but not awful – Similar reasons as 1) but the key difference is that consent is directly avoided. The focus of best interests is not the patient but the son

4) This would help the patient get back on track. A very appropriate thing to do – This is the best choice as the focus is on the patient care and treatment. it also promotes working in a trustworthy manner and protecting patient confidentiality.

5) Determine whether the child is at risk, but may take a while Appropriate, but not ideal – the key point to take away from this question and these questions in general is that the care of the patient is the main priority, be a good listener and understand the patient's concerns. Aim to maintain trust, integrity and patient confidentiality.

Now, here is another example to help internalise the key qualities that looked for in the SJT. This will be in the format of the 2nd style of questions:

A newborn baby is suffering from a congenital disease. Treatment is available, but if successful, would result in the baby having a severely reduced quality of life. The medical team has to decide what to do. How important is it to take into account the wishes of the baby itself when deciding how to respond to the situation?

Write down the key aspects of patient care that you think the situation wants you to look at

_____
_____
_____
_____
_____
_____
_____
_____
_____
_____
_____
_____
_____

Now here is the breakdown of the situation:

A newborn baby is suffering from a congenital disease. – Newborn baby, unable to consent to treatment, decisions must be made by the parents. Treatment is available, but if successful, would leave result in the baby having a severely reduced quality of life. – As a medical professional the best treatment must be provided, weighing the benefits and more importantly the harm of the treatments given to the patient. In this context it is the operation but this is also key in the possible side effects of the drugs. It is important that the patient can make decisions with full knowledge of what can go wrong. It is key that clinicians are effective listeners and communicators in order to address the patient's preference and concerns. The medical team has to decide what to do. – Whenever working in a team, it is important to be aware of any limitations and know how to work with members of other medical professionals to provide the best treatment for the patient. How important is it to take into account the wishes of the parents when deciding how to respond to the situation?

Questions: Circle the answer – for this format of questions, answers are given in terms of greatest importance.

1)   This is an important factor. If the quality of life is severely reduced it may be better to not attempt the treatment. However this is more of a factor for the family to decide on.

a)   Very important

b)   Important

c)   Of minor importance

d)   Not important at all

2)   The decision ultimately lies with the parents.

a)   Very important

b)   Important

c)   Of minor importance

d)   Not important at all

3)   The medical team should give their professional views, but ultimately the decision lies with the parents.

a)   Very important

b)   Important

c)   Of minor importance

d)   Not important at all

4)   This is an important factor as it could be a contributing factor to the parents when making the decision.

a)   Very important

b)   Important

c)   Of minor importance

d)   Not important at all

5)   The cost is not why the decision is being made, so is not an important factor.

a)   Very important

b) Important

c) Of minor importance

d) Not important at all

The model answers:

1) This is an important factor. If the quality of life is severely reduced it may be better to not attempt the treatment. However this is more of a factor for the family to decide on. Of minor importance – the assessment of the quality of life and its effect is not a valid one to make. The only goal is to provide the best treatment for the patient and the judgment of what effect this will have on the patient is the patient's decision or in this case the parent's choice. In this example, what seems important from clinical perspective might not be important to the patient. It could go against their belief system.

2) The decision ultimately lies with the parents. Very important- as mentioned above, the key is the patient. The parents are making the decision for the child because the child does not have the capacity to consent to the treatment. The decision of the parents must be respected as if it was the patient making the decision.

3) The medical team should give their professional views, but ultimately the decision lies with the parents. Of minor importance - personal views are not important. The only view that is important is that if those receiving the treatment. The healthcare professional's role is to provide the best care and treatment for the patient. It is the patient's choice on which treatment to choose.

4) This is an important factor as it could be an important factor to the parents when making the decision. Important – The parents are making the decision for the child, the considerations of the parents with regards to the quality of life is their choice to make.

5) The cost is not why the decision is being made, so is not an important factor. Not important at all – The cost of treatment is not important when providing the best treatment for the patient's health. The key role is of a medical professional is to maintain and improve life. Cost plays no part in this aspect.

Key take away points-

• The patient always comes first, respect their concerns and wishes about the treatment, in order to provide the treatment, which is best for them.

• Be honest and act with integrity.

• Be trustworthy; only break patient confidentiality if there is no other choice in terms of health of the patient.

• Have a respect for human life.

There are an enormous amount of resources for SJT in terms of scenarios available online. Also there are many different medical ethical guidelines that further expand on key qualities of a medical professional. It is recommended that these resources are used to help achieve a satisfactory band rating.

Hopefully at this stage the sections of UKCAT have become more familiar and approachable. The aim has been to develop candidates' skills to the point where questions are answered without putting much thought into it. Similar to the example of the child who learns to recognise words and what they mean, this stage of skill development is vital to understanding the sections of the UKCAT. The focus is to guide candidates to the point where they can master these skills and execute them naturally. There is a clear need to practice and practice for a minimum of four weeks. If this is not possible, the UKCAT may be more of a challenge. Using the skills highlighted in the breakdown will help candidates achieve a better score. A good source of extra UKCAT style questions to practice on can be found for free online. But, as stated before to really master these skills and prepare for the exam, try to use real life examples. This will help to build the right bridges to success and maintain a relaxed, flexible and adaptable approach that can handle virtually any of the questions that appear.

There are also other books that offer extra questions to practice on. Questions in the old format are not the most representative of what UKCAT 2014 is based upon. However, they are still useful to practice these skills and understand the process of how to handle these sections.

Keep coming back to the breakdown sections to master the skills required for the exams.

EXAM FORMAT

You are given 120 minutes (2 hours) for the UKCAT and 150 minutes (2 hours and 30 minutes) for the UKCAT special need test. This is a long time to stay focused; nonetheless, with the right preparation it can be done.

There is a maximum score of 900 for each section. Some universities use aggregate scores and have a cut- off score (generally over 600) , where candidates with a lower score than the cut- off are not considered; whereas, others require a certain minimum score in each of the sections in order to be considered. This varies from university to university and most colleges do not make public what method they use. For the test, remind yourself that each question counts and time wasted = lower scores.

We have kept it simple by homing in on important facts and information in order to give you a full picture of the exam. It's up to you to do the practice tests for each section and work hard up until your test date. We suggest that you focus on one section at a time to start with and really dig deep into why you're making mistakes and aim to improve with each question. There's absolutely no point in doing hundreds of questions without actually understanding the reasoning behind them. Even after you manage to complete this book, use real life situations and free online question in combination with the breakdown to get to where you want to be.

Using the 'one section at a time' strategy will enable you to identify early on where your strengths and weaknesses lie. For instance, if verbal reasoning is your weakest section, you can then start reading long articles in newspapers/online and see how much you can remember or how long it takes you to read it critically; the aim here is to identify your weakness early so that you can transform it into a strength. A low score in any one of the sections will lower your average and hence, it is important to tackle your weaknesses whilst keeping up your strengths. Most universities take into account an aggregate score and therefore, this technique will payoff in the long run.

UKCAT Breakdown Table

Subtest	Duration	Information	Test Items
Verbal Reasoning	22 minutes	11 passages of text need to be evaluated	44 items
Quantitative Reasoning	23 minutes	9 sets of tables, graphs, pie charts etc	36 items
Abstract Reasoning	14 minutes	13 sets of abstract shapes	55 items
Decision Analysis	34 minutes	1 box of codes	28 items
Situational Judgement Test	27 minutes	17 scenarios	71 items
Total Time	120 minutes		233

You are not allowed to take anything into the test. You will be provided with one/two laminated sheets to write on. An on-screen calculator will be provided which can be found on the top left hand corner of your screen

Some Tips before we get started on the practice questions

- You reap what you sow. It is imperative that you maximise your time until the test. We advise that you don't rely on how much you're peers are doing. Gauge your own capability and build a working pattern in order to develop accuracy and speed with your skills.

- Depending on how long you have until your test, you need to devise a daily study plan. Some candidates prefer to work a couple of hours every night, whereas others prefer to work five hours, every couple of days and then take a few days off. Do what works for you.

- Overcome your fear of failure, a mistakes is arguably your best resource. Back track from the correct answer to understand how to process the problem.

The following questions will be ordered in the sequence of the exam.

CHAPTER 3 : VERBAL REASONING

VERBAL REASONING

*Logical order of the passage and common
theme*

This section is the Verbal Reasoning practice question, we recommend you refresh your memory on how to approach this section on pages 20 - 27

What should you expect?

This section is designed to test your ability to read and critically analyse the information presented to you. There will be 11 passages of text, which can literally be about anything ranging from science topics to current affairs or even a passage from a storybook etc . You are expected to answer 44 questions based on these 11 passages. Remind yourself that they are not testing your pre-existing knowledge, but **rather** your ability to carefully analyse information.

Format 1

The question will be in the form of a statement and you have to choose whether the answers will be one of 'Yes'/'True, 'No'/'False' or 'Can't tell'.

Read the short passage below and determine the correct answer.

The production of smart phones and tablets continues to increase considerably, with demand particularly high in developed nations like Northern America, Tokyo and Britain. The rapid diffusion of technology and fast growing technological benefits are resulting in enhanced consumption, and the market is likely to quadruple over the next decade. With old players like Nokia who have now been left behind, while new contenders like Apple and Samsung take the lead, the future shows no signs of slowing down for this market and we can look forward to new entrants in this multi- billion industry.

Statement: Smart Phones and tablets are the fastest growing field in the Technological industry.
A.True   **B.** False   **C.** Can't Tell

True- if the statement can directly be justified by the passage, or if you were to put the statement in to the passage it wouldn't be out of place.

False- if there is something in the statement that is completely the opposite to what it states in the passage, or if you placed the sentence within the passage, it would outrightly stand out

Can't tell - Choose this option if there exists even **a shred of ambiguity** or uncertainty, particularly when the passage doesn't directly imply this but it could be true IF more information was given to you

Solution: According to the passage, "The production of smart phones and tablets continues to increase considerably, with demand ...is likely to quadruple over the next decade". Nonetheless, the passage does not explicitly state that smart phones and tablets are the fastest growing field in the technological industry. Based on current knowledge, we may be tempted to make assumptions and assume that the answer is true. However, **remember Rule #1**, the correct answer here is **'Can't Tell'**

Format 2

The options presented will take the form of an incomplete statement or a question, there will be four response options available. Students are required to choose the best or most suitable response. Candidates can only select a single response. Remember Rule # 1 and base your answer solely on the information provided in the text, so that you can confidently move on to the next, without any lingering doubt in your minds.

Some example questions are given below:

The author most likely agrees with all of the following except:
- Which of following claims is best supported by the passage?
- Which conclusion can be drawn from the passage?
- Which of the following assertions would strengthen/weaken 'some argument' that appeared in the passage?
- Which of the following statements is most/least likely to be true?

Simply understanding what the question requires of you is important in this test as time management is of the essence.

A helping hand before you crack on

1. This section requires a lot of concentration and being the first section, this works to your advantage.

2. If you are finding any one question extremely difficult, do not panic. Instead, eliminate the obvious incorrect answers, like what we have done in the breakdown, and then try and choose between the remaining two

3. The test is not negatively marked, so don't leave anything blank. Flag questions and come back to them. It's always better to make a wise guess rather than lose a mark.

4. You have 22 minutes (one minute for instruction) to complete 44 questions. So once you have read the instruction keep in mind that you have just under two minutes to do each question. This sounds like no time, but the more you practice you will realise that it is possible.

Verbal Reasoning Questions

Circle the correct answer

Stem 1

Below is an extract from an article about a new and upcoming restaurant:

Flaming Jack's is a modern and fun 40-cover American Diner, located in the heart of London's Soho. Themed specifically to appeal to our fashion-conscious, metropolitan clientele, Jack's is elegantly rustic, yet bright and inviting. Serving-up retro American favourites, our menu is appetizing and caters for all tastes. Quality, ethically sourced ingredients and a focus on food 'cooked to order' are a priority at Jack's.

Flaming Jack's is committed to providing the food that diners truly want- customisation is a key ingredient, made possible through our iPad-ordering system. With iPads mounted in a protective shell on each table, diners peruse the menu at their own convenience. Our custom-made app makes it simple and intuitive to modify your meal, with diners being able to select the main ingredients, sauces, toppings and sides as well as adding comments or special instructions for the chef such as allergies.

Orders are sent electronically to the kitchen and customers are notified of how long it will take before they can pick up their food themselves, halving the number of waiting staff needed. Our app will cater for the health-conscious, giving recommendations on the healthiest choices and displaying nutritional information for all items. Diners can pay immediately through each iPad, opting to pay the whole bill or splitting the bill between table members.

We will protect our brand name and logo, whilst our app and its associated intellectual property can be patented and we aim to do this as a matter of urgency.

Questions

1)The article is written by the prospective owners of Flaming Jack's.

    True   **False**   **Can't Tell**

2)According to the text, customers primarily want to be able to customise their food.

    True   **False**   **Can't Tell**

3)The text implies that customers wish to customise their food.

    True   **False**   **Can't Tell**

4)The iPad app will allow customers to change ingredients, sauces and portion sizes as well as other things.

    True   **False**   **Can't Tell**

5)The iPad system makes it cheaper for the restaurant to operate.

    True   **False**   **Can't Tell**

6)Flaming Jack's logo is of an American style.

    True   **False**   **Can't Tell**

7)One thing that is special about Flaming Jack's, is that customers are able to read the menu at their own convenience.

True   **False**   **Can't Tell**

8)Flaming Jack's provides healthy food.

True   **False**   **Can't Tell**

9)Customers will be able to communicate directly with the restaurant chef

True   **False**   **Can't Tell**

10)Which of the following is most likely to be true –

   a. The company's name and logo is in the process of being patented
   b. The restaurant will only require staff to collect payments
   c. People who eat in Soho tend to be fashion conscious.
   d. The restaurant will hire students.

Stem 2

Below is an extract from a restaurant business plan:

   'Rodriguez to go' is forecast to generate sales of £258,703 in Year 5 (2018). Net income before interest and tax for the full 2018 financial year is forecast at £46,719.

This assumes:
•The sales forecast is based on sales from the start up restaurant only and does not include the revenue from the intended sister restaurants to be opened in year 3-4.
•Sales volume growth is based on industry standard of 5% growth, for Birmingham restaurants in a similar sector of the industry.

   The projected profit indicates a breakeven point of just under 3000 meals a month, which we aim to do by providing an estimated 150 meals per day, giving a profit of £3600 per month.
We aim to gain positive cash balance by year 2. The cash flow forecast includes the assumption of sister restaurants having been opened in year 3 and 4. We hope to expand these restaurants to be larger than the start-up and in similar busy areas of Birmingham. We have therefore forecasted a cash balance of £700,000 by Year 5. This also includes the assumption that further Venture Capitalist funding will be sourced for the expansion of the restaurant to create a chain for franchising.
   We require £200,000 to open our start up restaurant 'Rodriguez to go'. This covers, according to affordable loss principles, the rent for one year (£50,000), the rent premium which allows for a lower rental rate throughout the year of (£100,000) and the fixtures and fittings cost (£50,000), including the fixed assets of technology and accessories.

Questions

1)'Rodriguez to go' will open in 2012.

True   **False**   **Can't Tell**

2)'Rodriguez to go' will close in 2018.

True   **False**   **Can't Tell**

3)'Rodriguez to go' will make a profit of £258,703 before tax in 2018.

True   **False**   **Can't Tell**

4)Sister restaurants will be open in year 3-4.

True   **False**   **Can't Tell**

5)If around 160 meals a day are sold, the restaurant will make a profit.

True   **False**   **Can't Tell**

6)The majority of the money required for start-up will be spent on rent.

True   **False**   **Can't Tell**

7)Similar restaurants all have a 5% growth.

True   **False**   **Can't Tell**

8)It is likely that the company will require further funding to create a restaurant chain.

True   **False**   **Can't Tell**

9)The company wish to open more than one sister restaurant in the future.

True   **False**   **Can't Tell**

10)Which is most likely false –

    a. 'Rodriguez to go' will open in 2013
    b. If sales volume growth is below 5%, the restaurant will lose money
    c. The company does not yet have venture capitalist funding
    d. The breakeven point is not 3000 meals per month.

Stem 3

A study summary is given below:

Research overview
   This paper explores the patient experience in a satellite dialysis unit, by evaluating service quality through the two proxies of waiting times and patient satisfaction.

Aims and objectives
   The aim of this study was to evaluate the service at Northwick Park satellite dialysis unit (NPSDU), and to propose areas of potential improvements. The four objectives of this study were:
(1) To **explore** which factors could affect patient experience in satellite dialysis units through the components of waiting times and patient satisfaction by conducting a narrative literature review

(2) To process map the patient pathway within NPSDU and **identify** factors which affect waiting times

(3) To **identify** factors which affect patient satisfaction at NPSDU

(4) To **propose** recommendations to improve service quality at NPSDU

Methods

To meet our objectives, we carried out two studies adopting a mixed methods approach. Study 1 involved process mapping the patient journey and carrying out structured observations. Study 2 analysed data from predetermined patient satisfaction questionnaires. Quantitative data analysis was conducted on data obtained from both studies, while comments obtained from study 2 were analysed qualitatively using thematic analysis.

Findings

Results showed significant associations between waiting times and type of transport, area of the unit, shift of the day, type of vascular access and mobility. Nurse seniority, however, was found to have no effect on waiting times. Patient satisfaction questionnaires indicated a high level of satisfaction within the unit; the only significant association found was between area of the unit and overall satisfaction with care.

Conclusions

Overall, our study found multiple factors to affect waiting times, but only one factor was found to affect satisfaction. The rationale underlying why these relationships may exist were limited by their somewhat speculative nature, but some were supported by our thematic analysis of patient questionnaires. All in all, this study helped calibrate future research into these important aspects of care.

Questions

1)There are four objectives, each with a different primary goal.

> **True**   **False**   **Can't Tell**

2)Each study contained different analysis.

> **True**   **False**   **Can't Tell**

3)Different areas had different waiting times.

> **True**   **False**   **Can't Tell**

4)The only association found in terms of satisfaction was to do with the area of the unit.

> **True**   **False**   **Can't Tell**

5)All the objectives were clearly met.

> **True**   **False**   **Can't Tell**

6)Senior nurses are just as capable as junior nurses.

> **True**   **False**   **Can't Tell**

7)The recommendations will improve service quality.

> **True**   **False**   **Can't Tell**

8)The recommendations may not improve service quality.

True   **False**   **Can't Tell**

9)The NPSDU operates in different areas.

True   **False**   **Can't Tell**

10)Which out of the following is true:

- a. Each study was analysed in the same way
- b. Study two could not have been analysed in a quantitative way
- c. Study two could have been analysed quantitatively
- d. Study one was solely based on waiting times.

Stem 4

Below is an extract from a research paper:

The NHS National Quality Board (NQB) recently established a working definition of patient experience, guiding its measurement across the NHS (NQB, 2011). A framework consisting of the eight constituent elements of patients' experience of NHS services was formed:

> - **Respect for patient-centred values, preferences, and expressed needs**
> - **Coordination and integration of care**
> - **Information, communication, and education**
> - **Physical comfort**
> - **Emotional support**
> - **Welcoming the involvement of family and friends**
> - **Access to care**

These recent developments in patient experience have guided our study, which focuses primarily on the domain of access to care, concerned with the waiting times of a patient journey.

Waiting times in this study encompasses any time between two steps in the patient journey, consecutive or otherwise. An important disambiguation here is that waiting times do not solely consist of time spent in the waiting room, it includes time spent receiving treatment for example.

Waiting times influence patient experience to the extent that aggression and anxiety are commonly resulting phenomena (Burns and Smyth, 2011). Burns and Smyth (2011) found that waiting times were a key trigger for aggression, accounting for 52% of aggression within the renal unit of St George's hospital.

The opportunity implicated in evaluating this aspect of patient experience is that through better understanding of waiting times we are able to implement strategies focusing on reducing the perceived or actual waiting times to improve patient experience. The NHS earnestly informs patients of the variation in waiting times in an attempt to manage patient expectations. Other means such as: greeting patients as they arrive; live updates about the number and types of cases that staff are presently dealing with; and clear signs explaining the different stages of treatment, are being implemented in certain hospitals to achieve the same end. Such methods to modify patients' perceptions are a powerful management tool to reduce perceived waiting times, and the resulting phenomena of anxiety and aggression discussed above.

Questions

1) The 8 constituent elements of patient experience have been written.

      True   **False**   **Can't Tell**

2) Access to care is the least important of all the elements of patient experience.

      True   **False**   **Can't Tell**

3) The paper was written in 2011.

      True   **False**   **Can't Tell**

4) The article primarily focuses on patient behaviour (aggression and anxiety).

      True   **False**   **Can't Tell**

5) Waiting times are the most important influence in patient experience.

      True   **False**   **Can't Tell**

6) Patient experience and waiting times are the focus of this passage.

      True   **False**   **Can't Tell**

7) Changing patient expectations is thought to help patients have a better experience.

      True   **False**   **Can't Tell**

8) We can assume that hospitals generally inform patients about varying waiting times.

      True   **False**   **Can't Tell**

9) St. George's hospital has a bad record of patient experience.

      True   **False**   **Can't Tell**

10) Which of the following is the most important for patient experience –

    a. Respect for patient-centred values, preferences, and expressed needs
    b. Access to care
    c. Waiting times
    d. It is not clear from the text

Below is an extract from a research study:

North West London runs the largest Haemodialysis (HD) programme in the UK with 1,400 patients being treated in eight satellite dialysis units based around one hub, the Imperial College Renal and Transplant Centre (ICRTC), situated in Hammersmith Hospital (Transplant Centre at the Hammersmith Hospital, 2013). Although the number of kidney donations is on the rise, 97.3% of ESRF patients in North-West London are on HD, 72.9% of which attend a satellite dialysis centre to receive treatment (Gilg et al., 2011).

Our study is based in NPSDU, located in West London, with an extremely diverse ethnic population. Compared to London and Great Britain as a whole, West London has a greater population of Asian and Afro-Caribbean ethnicities. Evidence suggests higher incidence of chronic kidney disease (CKD), a precursor to ESRF, among these ethnic minorities (Agarwal et al., 2005; Shulman and Hall, 1991).

At NPSDU, dialysis treatment is carried out from Monday to Saturday, with morning and afternoon shifts daily and an additional evening shift on Mondays, Wednesdays and Fridays.

The unit treats a population of 280 HD patients and has a total of 61 dialysis stations split up into six functionally separate areas. The seemingly bizarre layout of the unit is due to the fact that it was not built for purpose, and expanded incrementally to match growing demand over the years.

NPSDU, like most other satellite units, is nurse-led. While the resource savings enabled through increasing nurse roles has been well documented (RCN 2010), the potential trade-offs with quality in the domain of patient experience in a satellite dialysis unit has not. Therefore, scientific rigor should be applied before conclusions can be drawn on the quality implications in each of its applications, in this case satellite dialysis.

NPSDU provides insight into the drivers of quality at the largest satellite dialysis unit in the UK, which operates in the dominant hub and spoke model (Apira 2010). In studying a unit that lies within London, the area with the highest density of satellite dialysis spokes, we have access to a potentially rich source of data. Thus, we can gain insights into how effectively satellite units, with their unique characteristics, are in line with the NHS' future vision of high quality care for all.

Questions

1)North West London has the highest numbers of CKD in the UK.

True   **False**   **Can't Tell**

2)The article states that West London has the highest incidence of CKD.

True   **False**   **Can't Tell**

3)NPSDU has only morning and afternoon shifts from Monday to Saturday.

True   **False**   **Can't Tell**

4)There are approximately ten dialysis stations in each area of the unit.

True   **False**   **Can't Tell**

5)Quality of patient experience has not yet been looked into, with regards to the satellite unit.

True   **False**   **Can't Tell**

6)The article was written later than 2010 (inclusive).

True   **False**   **Can't Tell**

7)The author believes West London may not be the best place for a study.

True   **False**   **Can't Tell**

8)72.9% of ESRF patients go to a satellite dialysis centre.

True   **False**   **Can't Tell**

9)NPSDU has been generally well received by patients.

True   **False**   **Can't Tell**

10)Which of the following is true:

e. 72.9% of ESRF patients go to a satellite dialysis centre
f. 97.3% of patients on HD attend a satellite dialysis centre
g. Not all patients on HD attend a satellite dialysis centre
h. 72.9% of patients on HD in London go to a satellite dialysis centre

Stem 6

Below is an extract from a recent News article:

There exists much confusion and controversy amongst healthcare professionals as to the definition of telehealth; even the Department of Health (DOH) definition is subject to varied interpretation. The Royal Society of Medicine, quoting the DOH, defines telehealth as: "patient to clinician: vital signs and general condition monitoring such as blood pressure, weight, mental & physical state." Another recent paper (Hendy et al.) defines it as "the remote exchange of data between a patient, at home, and health care professionals, to assist in the management of an existing long-term condition i.e. COPD, diabetes, heart failure." The first notable inconsistency concerns location. The RSM definition does not specify a home environment, whilst the other does. Similarly, Hendy specifies long-term conditions only, whilst the RSM definition does not specify. The definition chosen in this review is the RSM DOH one, primarily due to its broad nature. By not stipulating the environment in which telehealth is delivered nor restricting to long-term conditions, a far broader range of telehealth services can be analysed and the scope of the review is much increased, whilst still being correct and relevant.

This review considers many forms of telehealth delivery such as telestroke and teleICU. Telecare is **not** considered in this systematic review and is defined as: "the remote, automatic monitoring of an individual's personal health and safety, i.e. mobility, and home environment." The term "telemedicine" is not currently used by the DOH and various definitions exist. Indeed, a 2007 study found 104 peer-reviewed definitions. It is similarly **not** considered in this review, although was included in the search strategy. "Remote care" is an umbrella term describing both telehealth and telecare (Hendy et al.), and was thus appropriately considered.

Questions

1)The paper has given two definitions for telehealth.

True   **False**   **Can't Tell**

2)The paper uses two definitions for telehealth.

| True | False | Can't Tell |

3)The Royal Society of Medicine definition for telehealth is the one used by most professionals.

| True | False | Can't Tell |

4)We can assume telecare is not part of telehealth.

| True | False | Can't Tell |

5)The author writes that telecare is not a form of telehealth.

| True | False | Can't Tell |

6)The paper does not define telemedicine.

| True | False | Can't Tell |

7)Remote care is a type of telehealth delivery.

| True | False | Can't Tell |

8)The author believes that the RSM definition for telehealth is the correct one.

| True | False | Can't Tell |

9)The author is studying how effective telehealth delivery is.

| True | False | Can't Tell |

10)Which of the following statements is false –

   a. Remote care relates to telehealth and telecare
   b. Telecare is a part of telehealth, but has not been considered
   c. Telecare is not part of telehealth
   d. Telemedicine has many different definitions.

Stem 7

Below is an extract from a recent online article:

Issues regarding implementation of telehealth programs such as training and installation have long been cited as potential pitfalls hindering large scale adoption. It is important to note that even those HCPs who are meant to deliver the service are no exception and hold similar thoughts.

A 2011 cross-sectional, qualitative study conducted in Scotland by Hanna et al. asked GPs their opinions regarding potential non face-to-face consultation methods. Most GPs felt that in order to use the new technologies, adequate frameworks would first have to be implemented including "support and training", along with clear legal advice. The sample size, whilst small at only 20, did cover the whole of Scotland. The study also stated that the results may be generalisable to the UK given the nationally negotiated General Practice contract is similar to Scotland. A key failing was that when discussing results, no specific figures were given, limiting the conclusions that can be drawn.

In a study of telemonitoring by heart failure nurses by Johnston et al., one nurse experienced significant difficulties during installation. She was concerned by her "lack of ability to undertake the installation." She also remarked that there was a lack of time to complete the installation. It must be noted that this was only one nurse, but, given the sample of four, is still significant. Apart from this small sample, a failing was that the nurses were not recruited explicitly for the purpose of this study, and they were interviewed as part of a larger research trial. This raises issues of selection bias, as no details have been given about the initial selection criteria for the larger trial. The nurses may have been selected initially due to their opinions on telehealth, for example. Another failing in the methodology is that the nurses were given the equipment and then left to their own devices. This caused problems such as nurses "cherry-picking" participants known to them and also performing the weight monitoring in a non-standardised fashion. These would potentially alter their opinions, limiting internal validity.

Questions

1) Large scale implementation of telehealth has not worked.
   True   **False**   **Can't Tell**

2) The study conducted in Scotland cannot be used as no specific figures were given when discussing results.
   True   **False**   **Can't Tell**

3) There was selection bias in the study by Johnson et al.
   True   **False**   **Can't Tell**

4) According to the author, it seems there were quite a few drawbacks to the Johnson et al. study.
   True   **False**   **Can't Tell**

5) Internal validity can be defined as how warranted a conclusion is.
   True   **False**   **Can't Tell**

6) 20 is a small sample size.
   True   **False**   **Can't Tell**

7) 4 is a small sample size.
   True   **False**   **Can't Tell**

8) The nurse in the Johnson et al. study was not able to perform the installation.
   True   **False**   **Can't Tell**

9) We can assume that telemonitoring is a part of telehealth.
   True   **False**   **Can't Tell**

10) We can assume the author believes what:

   a. The nurses should have been allocated participants randomly
   b. Then nurses were biased against telehealth
   c. Telehealth cannot be rolled out in a large scale
   d. The conclusions drawn from the Scotland study cannot be used.

Below is an extract from a study paper:

Face to face contact is often proclaimed as an invaluable tool in the practice of medicine. It is acknowledged to be the primary means of gathering information from a patient and an essential component of the doctor-patient relationship. With its ever increasing uptake, telehealth has the potential to irrevocably damage this age-old tradition, and thus it is again no surprise to find strong opinions in the literature.

In the Scotland paper Hanna et al., face-to-face consultation was considered central to practice by the GPs, and some did express some reservations about the potential detrimental effect of telehealth on face-to-face interaction. The main complaint was that telehealth would decrease the amount of time spent with the patient and would therefore lead to an inability to build and contribute to the breakdown of existing relationships with patients. Some GPs were more positive. They embraced the evolving doctor-patient relationship and "saw new technologies as providing an opportunity to build a new kind of relationship".

A strength of this paper is the authors' explicit attempts to recruit GPs with varying willingness to use technology, not just those enthusiastic about telehealth (minimising selection bias). They also noted that the study was focussed on the "microlevel communication" between doctor and patient, and recognised therefore that the results would be applicable regardless of the overall healthcare system of a country.

Questions

1)Face to face contact is an example of micro level communication.

True   **False**   **Can't Tell**

2)The use of telehealth has had a mixed response from GPs.

True   **False**   **Can't Tell**

3)Telehealth is becoming used more and more.

True   **False**   **Can't Tell**

4)Face to face contact is the most important way to gain evidence from a patient.

True   **False**   **Can't Tell**

5)The author believes it is important to use participants who have differing views on the subject.

True   **False**   **Can't Tell**

6)An example of selection bias would be using just GPs who were positive about telehealth.

True   **False**   **Can't Tell**

7)Microlevel communication occurs across the healthcare system.

True   **False**   **Can't Tell**

8)Overall, more GPs were against telehealth than for it.

True   **False**   **Can't Tell**

9)Overall, more GPs were for telehealth than against it.

True   False   Can't Tell

10) Which of the following is most likely to be false :

   a. The paper did not contain much selection bias
   b. The doctor-patient relationship is changing
   c. The paper did not contain any selection bias
   d. The doctor-patient relationship may be changed with this new technology.

Verbal reasoning Answers

Stem 1

1) **True**. This is a tricky question, even though there is not a specific author, there is a reference to 'our menu'. "We will protect our brand name and logo" this line suggests ownership of the brand.

2) **False**. There is word play in the questions, although the text says 'Flaming Jack's is committed to providing to providing the food that diners truly want- customisation is a key ingredient' The questions states 'primarily want to be able to customise their food' Indicating that the customer want to customise the food, but there is no information that this is what the customer 'primarily wants'.

3) **True**. Here the question states the ' customers want to be able to customise their food' which matches the vision of the restaurant in 'providing the food that diners truly want- customisation is a key ingredient'.

4) **False**. 'app makes it simple and intuitive to modify your meal, with diners being able to select the main ingredients, sauces, toppings and sides as well as adding comments or special instructions for the chef such as allergies' The app will not allow customers to change portion sizes.

5) **True**. 'halving the number of waiting staff needed'. The restaurant requires less staff, so this makes it cheaper.

6) **Can't Tell**. There is no information on what the logo looks like.

7) **False**. This a feature of the restaurant and a benefit to the restaurant as stated : 'iPads mounted in a protective shell on each table, diners peruse the menu at their own convenience'. It does not say that this is unique or special to Flaming Jack's.

8) **Can't Tell**. The text states: 'Our app will cater for the health-conscious' Flaming Jack's allows customers to see the healthiest options, but there is no information on how healthy food is.

9) **False**. 'special instructions for the chef' Customers will be able to communicate with the chef by writing on the iPad app. But not directly with the chef as the question specifies.

10) **C. People who eat in Soho tend to be fashion conscious.** This is the true statement because as the text says 'Themed specifically to appeal to our fashion-conscious, metropolitan clientele'. We can assume that this is linked.

why are the other options most likely false?

a. The company's name and logo is in the process of being patented -This is false because 'We will protect our brand name and logo, whilst our app and its associated intellectual property can be patented' It is the app that they're looking to patent

b. & d. The restaurant will only require staff to collect payments & The restaurant will hire students - There is no information in the passage to specify this

Stem 2

1) **False**. ' 'Rodriguez to go' is forecast to generate sales of £258,703 in Year 5 (2018)' It will open in 2013, This is a 5 year forecast ending at 2018, 2018 - 5 = 2013.

2) **False**. There is nothing to suggest that the restaurant will close in 2018.

3) **False**. 'generate sales of £258,703' , not profit.

4) **Can't Tell**. 'the intended sister restaurants to be opened in year 3-4', but this is a future prediction.

5) **True**. 'estimated 150 meals per day, giving a profit of £3600 per month.', so 160 meals will yield profit.

6) **True**. 'the rent for one year (£50,000), the rent premium which allows for a lower rental rate throughout the year of (£100,000)' which in total is £150,000 of the £200,000 will be spent on rent or the rent premium.

7) **Can't Tell**. 'Sales volume growth is based on industry standard of 5% growth', but we do not know if every restaurant achieves this exact figure (or not).

8) **True**. 'This also includes the assumption that further Venture Capitalist funding will be sourced for the expansion of the restaurant to create a chain for franchising.'.

9) **True**. The text states' We hope to expand these restaurants to be larger than the start-up' restaurants rather than restaurant, indicating more than one.

10) **b. If sales volume growth is below 5%, the restaurant will lose money** We cannot say this is true, as we have not been given exact figures for profit margins.

Why are the other options true?

a. 'Rodriguez to go' will open in 2013 – Same rationale to the answer as 1)

c. The company does not yet have venture capitalist funding
   'This also includes the assumption that further Venture Capitalist funding'

d. The breakeven point is not 3000 meals per month. – 'a breakeven point of just under 3000 meals a month'

Stem 3

1) **False**. There are four objectives but three primary goals, explore, identify, and propose.

2) **False**. 'Quantitative data analysis was conducted on data obtained from both studies, while comments obtained from study 2 were analysed qualitatively using thematic analysis.' Both studies were quantitatively analysed.

3) **True**. 'significant associations between waiting times and type of transport, area of the unit' The fact that there was an association between different areas and waiting times means that this must be true.

4) **Can't Tell**. There was an association between waiting time and area. We do not know the association in terms of satisfaction.

5) **False**. We cannot see evidence of any recommendations.

6) **Can't Tell**. '. Nurse seniority, however, was found to have no effect on waiting times' There is no information on the capability of the nurses.

7) **Can't Tell**. We do not know if the recommendations will be implemented and if so whether they will be effective or not.

8) **True.** This is a possibility, as we cannot know what will happen in the future.
9) **True.** 'Results showed significant associations between waiting times and type of transport, area of the unit' We know there is a correlation between waiting time and area of unit. So the NPSDU must operate in different areas.
10) ; **Study two could have been analysed quantitatively;** 'Quantitative data analysis was conducted on data obtained from both studies'. The answers could have been therefore analysed in this way.

Why are the other options false?

    a. Each study was analysed in the same way – Same rationale to the answer as 1)
    b. Study two could not have been analysed in a quantitative way - rationale to answer 10)
    d. Study one was solely based on waiting times. – 'Study 1 involved process mapping the patient journey and carrying out structured observations. Study 2 analysed data from predetermined patient satisfaction questionnaires.' Neither of the studies focused solely on waiting time

Stem 4

1) **False.** The box only states 7 of the 8.
2) **Can't Tell**. Although there is 7 of the 8 elements in the box, it isn't ranked, there is no information on which is the most important.
3) **Can't Tell.** Although the references are from 2011, this does not necessarily mean the paper was written then.
4) **False.** 'Burns and Smyth (2011) found that waiting times were a key trigger for aggression, accounting for 52% of aggression within the renal unit of St George's hospital ' this is a quote used to establish the link between waiting times and aggression. This is only a small constituent of the article.
5) **Can't Tell.** Combieing with the rationale from 2) that the influences aren't ranked in importance highlights there is no information on whether this is the most important influence..
6) **True.** The bulk of the text is dedicated to one of these two points, also 'which focuses primarily on the domain of access to care, concerned with the waiting times of a patient journey' highlights the aims of the study including waiting times, so we can take this to be true.
7) **True.** 'Other means such as: greeting patients as they arrive; live updates about the number and types of cases that staff are presently dealing with;....Such methods to modify patients' perceptions are a powerful management tool to reduce perceived waiting times' This quote highlights that importance of patient perception and expectation in the patient experience. Therefore we can deduce that this is true.
8) **True.** 'The NHS earnestly informs patients of the variation in waiting times' The article says the NHS does this, so it is safe to assume this is the case.
9) **Can't Tell.** 'within the renal unit of St George's hospital' There is no information given on patient experience as a whole at St. George's.
10) **It is not clear from the text.** The text does not contain any information on which is the most important.

Why are the other options not the most important for patient experience?

The other three options are elements of patient care and as stated previously we do not know what is most important

Stem 5

1) **Can't Tell.** 'North West London runs the largest Haemodialysis (HD) programme in the UK' this doesn't necessarily mean that CKD is the highest in North West London. Although 'Evidence suggests higher incidence of chronic kidney disease (CKD), a precursor to ESRF, among these ethnic minorities' and 'Compared to London and Great Britain as a whole, West London has a greater population of Asian and Afro-Caribbean ethnicities' this does not necessarily mean it has the highest numbers.
2) **False.** The article states that the types of population found in West London have a higher incidence, but does not say that West London itself has the highest incidence.
3) **False.** 'an additional evening shift on Mondays, Wednesdays and Fridays'
4) **Can't Tell.** Although there is 'a total of 61 dialysis stations split up into six functionally separate areas', we do not know if they are evenly spread or not.
5) **True.** 'While the resource savings enabled through increasing nurse roles has been well documented (RCN 2010), the potential trade-offs with quality in the domain of patient experience in a satellite dialysis unit has not.' - that the trade off with quality in the domain of patient experience is not well documented.
6) **True.** The most recent reference is from 2011, so the article must have been written in 2011 or later.
7) **False.** 'Our study is based in NPSDU, located in West London, with an extremely diverse ethnic population. Compared to London and Great Britain as a whole' The author writes that West London has a potentially rich source of data.
8) **False.** '97.3% of ESRF patients in North-West London are on HD, 72.9% of which attend a satellite dialysis centre to receive treatment' 72.9% of patients on HD go to a satellite dialysis centre.
9) **Can't Tell.** There is no information on patient satisfaction.
10) **Not all patients on HD attend a satellite dialysis centre** 72.9% of patients on HD do, so not all of them.

Why are the other options false?

a. 72.9% of ESRF patients go to a satellite dialysis centre – Same rationale as 8)
b. 97.3% of patients on HD attend a satellite dialysis centre – '97.3% of ESRF patients in North-West London are on HD, 72.9% of which attend a satellite dialysis centre to receive treatment'
d. 72.9% of patients on HD in London go to a satellite dialysis centre – 'patients in North-West London'. We do not know the information for the whole of London

Stem 6

1) **True.** The RSM definition '"patient to clinician: vital signs and general condition monitoring such as blood pressure, weight, mental & physical state." ' and the definition by Hendy et al "the remote exchange of data between a patient, at home, and

health care professionals, to assist in the management of an existing long-term condition' .

2) **False.** 'The definition chosen in this review is the RSM DOH one' The paper chooses the RSM definition.

3) **Can't Tell.** There is no information on whether the RSM definition is the most widely used.

4) **True.** ' "Remote care" is an umbrella term describing both telehealth and telecare' we can assume they are separate.

5) **False.** 'Telecare is **not** considered in this systematic review' The author does not specifically write that Telecare is not a form of telehealth.

6) **True.** The paper says there are '104 peer-reviewed definitions', but does not give a specific one to define telemedicine.

7) **False.** This is just a play with words. '"Remote care" is an umbrella term describing both telehealth and telecare' Telehealth is a type of remote care.

8) **Can't Tell.** The author does not state which is correct, just that he/she will use the RSM 'primarily due to its broad nature'.

9) **Can't Tell.** There is no information on what aspect of telehealth is being studied.

10) **b. Telecare is a part of telehealth, but has not been considered**. As stated in the rationale of 4) Telecare is not a part of telehealth.

Why are the other statements true?

 e. Remote care relates to telehealth and telecare - '"Remote care" is an umbrella term describing both telehealth and telecare'

 c. Telecare is not part of telehealth - '"Remote care" is an umbrella term describing both telehealth and telecare'

 d. Telemedicine has many different definitions. – '"telemedicine" is not currently used by the DOH and various definitions exist. Indeed, a 2007 study found 104 peer-reviewed definitions'

 Stem 7

1) **False.** The text merely states 'potential pitfalls hindering large scale adoption.' – implementation has not yet happened.

2) **False.** 'A key failing was that when discussing results, no specific figures were given, limiting the conclusions that can be drawn.' The study's conclusions are limited but still can be used.

3) **Can't Tell.** 'This raises issues of selection bias, as no details have been given about the initial selection criteria for the larger trial.' There may have been selection bias, but we do not know this for sure.

4) **True.** The author lists several problems in paragraph about the Johnston et al study.

5) **Can't Tell.** We do not know what the definition is based on the text only. There is a reference to internal validity 'This caused problems such as nurses "cherry-picking" participants known to them and also performing the weight monitoring in a non-standardised fashion. These would potentially alter their opinions, limiting internal validity' but no clear definition is given.

6) **True.** The author states this. – ' The sample size, whilst small at only 20'

7) **True.** The author states this. – 'given the sample of four, is still significant. Apart from this small sample'

8) **Can't Tell.** 'She was concerned by her "lack of ability to undertake the installation." She also remarked that there was a lack of time to complete the installation.' – there's no specific information stating if the installation was completed or not.

9) **True.** In the beginning of the 3rd paragraph it was started 'In a study of telemonitoring by heart failure nurses'. Later in the paragraph, The author then goes on to write that 'The nurses may have been selected initially due to their opinions on telehealth' so it's safe to presume telemonitoring is a part of telehealth.

10) **a. The nurses should have been allocated participants randomly**. The author says 'problems such as nurses "cherry-picking" participants known to them and also performing the weight monitoring in a non-standardised fashion. These would potentially alter their opinions' It's safe to say the author believes the nurses should have been allocated participants.

Why are the other options NOT what the author believes?

 b. Then nurses were biased against telehealth –' The nurses may have been selected initially due to their opinions on telehealth' The author is not sure.

 c. Telehealth cannot be rolled out in a large scale – 'potential pitfalls hindering large scale adoption this doesn't mean it can't happen

 d. The conclusions drawn from the Scotland study cannot be used. – 'the results may be generalisable to the UK'

Stem 8

Face to face contact is often proclaimed as an invaluable tool in the practice of medicine. It is acknowledged to be the primary means of gathering information from a patient and an essential component of the doctor-patient relationship. With its ever increasing uptake, telehealth has the potential to irrevocably damage this age-old tradition, and thus it is again no surprise to find strong opinions in the literature.

In the Scotland paper Hanna et al., face-to-face consultation was considered central to practice by the GPs, and some did express some reservations about the potential detrimental effect of telehealth on face-to-face interaction. The main complaint was that telehealth would decrease the amount of time spent with the patient and would therefore lead to an inability to build and contribute to the breakdown of existing relationships with patients. Some GPs were more positive. They embraced the evolving doctor-patient relationship and "saw new technologies as providing an opportunity to build a new kind of relationship".

A strength of this paper is the authors' explicit attempts to recruit GPs with varying willingness to use technology, not just those enthusiastic about telehealth (minimising selection bias). They also noted that the study was focused on the "microlevel communication" between doctor and patient, and recognised therefore that the results would be applicable regardless of the overall healthcare system of a country.

1) **Can't Tell**. 'an invaluable tool in the practice of medicine' Although we can probably assume this, there is no link between these two in stated in the text.

2) **True**. 'some did express some reservations about the potential detrimental effect of telehealth on face-to-face interaction.' and 'Some GPs were more positive'

3) **True**. The texts states 'With its ever increasing uptake, telehealth has the potential to irrevocably damage this age-old tradition' implying it is getting used more and more.

4) **True.** It is described as 'primary means of gathering information from a patient', the key word is primary which then relates to most important.

5) **True.** The author states this in the text: 'A strength of this paper is the authors' explicit attempts to recruit GPs with varying willingness to use technology'

6) **True.** Although we may know the answer from prior knowledge, it is key not to use it and check within the text 'A strength of this paper is the authors' explicit attempts to recruit GPs with varying willingness to use technology, not just those enthusiastic about telehealth (minimising selection bias).' Implies just using GPs who were pro telehealth would be bias

7) **True.** The author states, 'the study was focused on the "micro-level communication" between doctor and patient, and recognised therefore that the results would be applicable regardless of the overall healthcare system of a country' – we can therefore assume this to be true.

8) **Can't Tell.** There is no information on figures.

9) **Can't Tell.** There is no information on figures.

10) **c. The paper did not contain any selection bias**. – Is most likely to be false because we cannot say for sure if the paper contained absolutely no selection bias, 'A strength of this paper is the authors' explicit attempts to recruit GPs with varying willingness to use technology' the authors went out recruiting GPs on willingness to use technology so this is most likely to be false.

Why were the other options most likely true?

a.   The paper did not contain much selection bias – 'A strength of this paper is the authors' explicit attempts to recruit GPs with varying willingness to use technology, not just those enthusiastic about telehealth (minimising selection bias).'

b.   The doctor-patient relationship is changing - 'They embraced the evolving doctor-patient relationship and "saw new technologies as providing an opportunity to build a new kind of relationship".'

d.   The doctor-patient relationship may be changed with this new technology. – ' "saw new technologies as providing an opportunity to build a new kind of relationship".'

CHAPTER 4 : QUANTITATIVE REASONING

QUANTITATIVE REASONING

Your ability to recall your long term
memory through calculation of numbers

This section is the Quantitative Reasoning practice question, we recommend you refresh your memory on how to approach this section on pages 4-14.

What is expected of you?

This subtest assesses your ability to use mathematical skills to solve problems. You will be given 23 minutes to solve 36 items which may involve interpreting graphs, tables, charts or statements. It is assumed that all candidates are of a reasonable level from GCSE Maths, and therefore, we advise that if students struggle in this area, they should prioritise practising this subtest over the others. Otherwise, a low score here will bring down your average result. Because of all the analysis and data interpretation required for this section, it is important to keep an eye on the clock and move swiftly from one question to the next.

Top tips!!

1. Only use a calculator if you really need to. Most students spend unnecessary time on the calculator to double check answers; this time could be preciously spent on other questions. So get enough practice to feel confident with your answer choices.
2. Practice using the on screen calculator on the mock tests provided by www.ukcat.ac.uk

3. If nerves and the pressure get to you, Don't panic! Make a wise guess by ruling out answers that are in the wrong units or too far from what could be correct (remember there is no negative marking)
4. Make sure your answers are in the correct units and to the right decimal place as specified by the question; this is often an easy error that can be avoided.
5. Regularly practice your numerical skills and mental arithmetic using websites and other resources, so that nothing surprises you on the data

Quantitative reasoning questions

QUESTION 1

A man wants to take his wife and three young children on holiday to somewhere hot and sunny. He is comparing flight and hotel prices to several destinations.

Flights (return)								
	Sun Tours		Easyfly		British Airlines		London Travel	
	Adult	Child	Adult	Child	Adult	Child	Adult	Child
Algarve	£200	£120	£190	£120	£200	£100	£160	£120
Barcelona	£160	£100	£160	£90	£170	£85	£150	£100
Rome	£225	£100	£230	£105	£250	£125	£200	£150
Crete	£280	£140	£260	£150	£280	£140	£230	£175

Hotels (5 nights for whole family)				
	Sun Tours	QuickFind	Sun and Sand	London Travel
Algarve	£550	£520	£600	£525
Barcelona	£600	£590	£630	£600
Rome	£575	£575	£600	£595
Crete	£550	£500	£490	£500

Sun Tours offers a 10% discount on the total price if flights and hotels are both booked through their company, whilst London Travel offers £50 cash-back if flights and hotels are both booked through their company.

1) How much a holiday, with his family, to the Algarve cost through Sun Tours?

   a. £1310 b. £760 c. £550 d.£1179 e. £1200

2) What is the cheapest price he can take his family to Rome for?

   a. £1192.50 b. £1325 c. £1395 d. £1200 c. £1300

3) What is the cheapest price he can get return flights to Rome if he takes only his wife?

   a. £450 b. £400 c. £405 d. £350 e. £460

4) What is the difference in price if to go to Barcelona with his family, if he booked through Easyfly and Sun and Sand, compared with British Airlines and QuickFind?

   a. £1185 b. £1220 c. £15 d. £20 e. £35

5) Easyfly are having a 15% sale on flights. What is the new price of flights to take his family to Crete?

   a. £824.50 b. £970 c. £1141 d. £900 e. £950

6) What is the difference in price if he were to use London Travel for flights and hotels to Barcelona, compared with using London Travel for flights and QuickFind for hotels to book a holiday with his family?

   a. £50 b. £1200 c. £40 d. £10 e. £1190

7) What is the cheapest price he can take his family on holiday to Crete for?

   a.£1460 b.£1377 c. £1530 d. £1435 e. £1480

8) If Sun Tours reduced their discount to 5%,what would the difference between the old and new price of taking a holiday, with his family, to the Algarve be?

   a. £50 b. £1244.50 c. £1179 d. £65.50 e. £25

9) What is the difference in price between Algarve and Barcelona if he books completely through London Travel?

   a.£50 b. £100 c. £5 d. £57.50 e. £60

10) What is the cheapest place he can go to with Sun Tours?

   a. None b. Algarve. c. Barcelona d. Rome e. Crete

   QUESTION 2

Below are the prices of various items in a wholesale T-Shirt warehouse.It is recommended that all Jumpers are sold at 3x wholesale price. If the same item is ordered but with different graphics, then the discounts are eligible on the total order.

Plain white Jumpers
£3.00 per item up to 50 items ordered.
£2.75 per item if between 51 and 100 items are ordered.
£2.50 per item if between 101 and 200 items are ordered.
£2.25 per item for 201+ items ordered.

Plain coloured Jumpers
£3.50 per item up to 50 items ordered.
£3.30 per item if between 51 and 100 items are ordered.
£3.10 per item if between 101 and 200 items are ordered.
£2.90 per item for 201+ items ordered.

To add black Graphics
£1 per item for white Jumpers.
£1.50 per item for coloured Jumpers.

To add coloured Graphics
£2 per item for white Jumpers.
£2.50 per item for coloured Jumpers.

1) Someone wishes to buy 55 plain white Jumpers. How much will this cost?

   a .£163.75 b. £151.25 c. £161.25 d. £153.75 e. £152.15

2) A retailer wishes to buy 50 plain white Jumpers and 100 plain coloured Jumpers. How much will this cost?

   a. £480 b. £447.50 c. £460 d. £467.50 e.£470

3) Someone wishes to buy 100 plain white Jumpers with black graphics, and 100 plain white Jumpers with coloured graphics. How much will this cost?

   a. £850 b. £910 c.£950 d, £710 e. £810

4) How much profit can a retailer make on 125 plain coloured Jumpers, if sold at the recommended price?

   a.£387.50 b. £1162.50 c. £775 d. £825 e. £725

5) A retailer buys 60 plain white Jumpers, and 75 plain coloured Jumpers with black graphics. He sells most of the items, but has 10 white and 15 coloured Jumpers left over. What was the profit/loss?

a. £1050 b. -£1050 c. £1276.50 d. £751.50 e. -£751.50

6) How much will it cost to buy 300 plain coloured jumpers, half with black graphics and half with coloured graphics?

a.£1530 b. £930 c. £1230 d. £1470 e. £870

7) A shop buys 200 plain white Jumpers, and 100 plain coloured Jumpers. However the shop goes bankrupt, and can only sell them at 1.5x the value they were bought for. What is the difference in profit made compared with if they were sold at 3x the wholesale price.

a.£415 b. £1,140 c. £380 d. £400 e. £1245

8) A retailer sells 200 white Jumpers with coloured graphics for a total of £1500 profit. How much must the retailer have been selling each Jumper for?

a. £12 b. £7.50 c. £5 d. £9.75 e. £7.25

9) What is the cost of buying 60 plain white Jumpers with coloured graphics, and 80 coloured Jumpers with black graphics?

a.£653 b. £669 c. £709 d. £769 e. £753

10) The wholesaler places a 10% discount on all orders. What is the difference between buying 75 plain white Jumpers and 75 plain coloured Jumpers before, compared with now?

a.£45.38 b. £45.36 c. £45.37 d. £408.39 e. £408.38

QUESTION 3

Every year, 5 people take part in a sponsored swim for charity. Below is a table showing the amount they each swam over a 5 year period (In lengths).

Person	2008	2009	2010	2011	2012
Duncan	750	760	770	780	790
James	300	320	340	360	360
Katie	500	525	550	575	550
Chris	600	580	580	540	560
Kate	700	700	700	700	710

1) If each length is 25m, how much has Kate swum in total?

a.87,500 b. 67,500 c. 87,750 d. 3,510 e. 3,500

2) If each length is 25m, how much did the group swim altogether in 2010?

a.73,250 b. 73,750 c. 73,000 d. 74,000 e. 73,500

3) If the group raised £15,675 in 2008, and they all charged the same per length, how much were they sponsored per length?

   a.£5 b. £6 c. 55p d. 60p e. £5.50

4) What proportion of the total lengths that year did Katie swim in 2009?

   a. 0.18 b. 0.19 c. 0.24 d. 0.25 e. 0.22

5) If each length is 25m, what was the average amount swum in 2011?

   a. 591 b. 14,775 c. 14,750 d. 15,000 e. 590

6) If they each asked for £6 per length in 2012, how much did they raise in total?

   a. £17,730 b. £17,760 c. £2,960 d. £17,820 e. £2,970

7) What was the most anyone swam in the whole 5 year period?

   a. Duncan b. James c. Katie d. Chris e. Kate

8) Who swam the least over 5 years?

   a. Duncan b. James c. Katie d. Chris e. Kate

9) What was the percentage change in Duncan's total number of lengths from 2010 to 2012?

   a. 2.2% b. 2.3% c. 2.4% d. 2.5% e. 2.6%

10) If each length is 25m, how much less did Chris swim in 2010 compared with 2012?

   a.1000m b. 200m c. 500m d. 50m e. 20m

QUESTION 4

Jayden is an artist. She does caricatures for fixed prices. A small caricature costs £10, whilst a large costs £16.

1) What is the difference in price between three small and two large caricatures?

   a. £28 b. £30 c.£2 d. £32 e. £8

2) A tourist asks Jayden to draw 5 small caricatures for his children, and 3 large ones for him, his wife, and his brother. How much does this cost the tourist in total?

   a. £48 b. £50 c. £98 d. £110 e. £194

3) Another tourist asks Jayden to draw 4 small caricatures and 4 large ones. He decides to tip her 5%. How much does this cost the tourist in total?

   a. £109.20 b. £109 c. £104 d. £99 e. £134.40

4) Jayden uses £2 worth of material for small caricatures, and £3 for large ones. If she draws 20 small and 15 large caricatures, how much profit does she make?

   a. £440 b. £370 c. £335 d. £355 e. £85

5) Jayden uses £2 worth of material for small caricatures, and £3 for large ones. If she needs to draw 13 small

and 11 large caricatures, how much will the material cost?

   a. £48 b. £72 c. £61 d. £60 e. £59

6) Jayden believes that the day will be busy, so raises her prices by £1 for small and £2 for large caricatures. She expects that she will have to draw 30 small and 20 large ones. How much money will she receive?

   a. £620 b. £690 c. £570 d. £500 e. £600

7) Jayden believes that the day will be busy, so raises her prices by £1 for small and £2 for large caricatures. On average, she draws 20 small and 15 large caricatures per day. However, due to her increased price, she only draws 15 small and 10 large caricatures. What is the difference in profit on an average day compared to today?

   a. £120 b. £145 c. £160 d. £175 e. £95

8) Jayden decides to pin some examples on a board. A small caricature is 20cm long by 15cm wide. A large caricature is 40cm by 30cm. If she wishes to pin 3 small ones side by side, how wide a board will she need?

   a. 45cm b. 60cm c. 90cm d. 120cm e. 75cm

9) Jayden decides to pin some examples on a board. A small caricature is 20cm long by 15cm wide. A large caricature is 40cm by 30cm. If she decides to pin 3 large ones side by side, and 4 small ones underneath side by side, how big will the board need to be?

   a. 90 x 60 b. 60 x 90 c. 120 x 45 d. 45 x 120 e. 45 x 90

10) Jayden gives a 20% discount to her first customer, who orders a large caricature. What will the caricature cost the customer?

   a. £14.40 b. £3.60 c. £16 d. £12.80 e. £3.20

QUESTION 5

Shampoo

Colour guard plus, a shampoo producer, produces a new range of shampoo with new colour protection technology. The shampoo is only available in two sizes, 250ml and 500ml. They cost £5 and £7.50 respectively

---

1. What is the cheapest price value of 2750ml of this product?

   a. £40.50   b. £55   c. £42.50 d. £51.50 e. £50

2. Comparing 2 x 250ml bottles to 500ml what is the percentage increase of cost comparing the 250 bottles to the 500ml?

   a. 50% b. 33% c.45% d. 26% e. 30%

3. A local drug store offer a 2 for 1 offer on the 250ml bottles, how much would you save if you wanted 2000ml of the shampoo?

   a. £30   b. £40 c. £35 d. £20 e. £25

4. Another store sells 360 250ml bottles and 120 500ml bottles, what is the ratio of 250ml to 500ml bottles sold in the store?

   a.4:1   b. 160:50 c. 3:1 d. 2.5:1 e.5:1

QUESTION 6

Motorcycle

Alex is a professional racer who races in the World Championships, He owns a prototype motorcycle. This motorcycle can go from 0-60mph in 3 seconds, 60-100mph in 3.5 seconds and steadily increase of 10mph per second in a linear fashion from 100-150mph and after that it takes 15seconds to reach the top speed of 180mph.

---

1) How long does it take him to reach 165mph?

   a. 19 seconds   b. 11.5 seconds c. 13 seconds d. 17.5 seconds e. 21seconds

2) He accelerates for 8 seconds, what is his speed?

   a. 120mph   b. 110mph c. 125mph d. 122.5mph e. 115mph

3) The motorcycle is restricted to 130mph, how long will it take before the restrictions takes place?

   a. 12seconds   b. 8.5seconds c. 9.5seconds d. 10seconds e. 9seconds

4) Another motorcycle takes 5 seconds to reach 90mph how many seconds is it faster than Alex's motorcycle? —

   a. 1second   b. 0.5seconds   c. 1.5seconds   d. 0.75seconds   e. Can't tell

> **Cafe**
>
> **Joe's café is a café in Smallingham. His main sellers are the: Full English breakfast, Cheeseburgers and The Joe's special. The café makes a profit of £4 per Full English breakfast, £2.50 per Cheeseburgers and £5.50 per The Joe's special. On average the café sales 8 Full English breakfast, 15 Cheeseburgers and 7 The Joe's special per day**

1) Today has been a busy day, he sales 15 Full English breakfast, 21 Cheeseburgers and 10 The Joe's special. How much profit has me made just considering these three items?

   a. £167.50   b. £155.50   c. £160.50   d. £157.50   e. £165.50

2) The owner sources a new supplier of ingredients that increase his profit of £1 per Full English breakfast, £0.50 per Cheeseburgers and £2 per The Joe's special. What is the percentage increase in profit on average per day?

   a. 28%   b. 27%   c. 25%   d. 9.30%   e. 26%

3) What this the ratio of the profit of Full English breakfast, Cheeseburger compared to The Joe's special on average per day?

   a. £32 : £37 : £38.50 **b.** £15 : £30.50 : £38.50 **c.** £38.50 : £37.50 : £32 **d.** £32 : £37.50 : £38.50 **e.** £37.50 : £32 : £38.50

4) The café excels under new management, now on average the café sales 20 Full English breakfast what is ratio compared to the previous average?

   a. 5:2   b. 2:5   c. 40:8   d. 2:1   e. 2:4

Quantitative Reasoning Answers

1) How much a holiday to the Algarve cost through Sun Tours?

d. £1179 - Flights for 2 adults + 3 children = £760. Add hotel price = £1310. Minus 10% = £1179

2) What is the cheapest price he can take his family to Rome for?

a. £1192.50 - With Sun Tours, Flights for 2 adults + 3 children = £750. Add hotel price = £1325. Minus 10% = £1192.50

3) What is the cheapest price he can get return flights to Rome if he takes only his wife?

B. £400 - With London Travel, flights for 2 adults = £400. No cash-back or discount as no hotel booking.

4) What is the difference in price if to go to Barcelona if he booked through Easyfly and Sun and Sand, compared with British Airlines and QuickFind?

e. £35 - Easyfly for 2 adults + 3 children = £590. Add to Sun and Sand hotel = £1220. British Airlines for 2 adults + 3 children = £595. Add to QuickFind Hotel = £1185. Difference is £35.

5) Easyfly are having a 15% sale on flights. What is the new price of flights to take his family to Crete?

a. £824.50 - Easyfly flights for 2 adults + 3 children = £970. Minus 15% = £824.50

6) What is the difference in price if he were to use London Travel for flights and hotels to Barcelona, compared with using London Travel for flights and QuickFind for hotels?

c. £40 - London Travel flights for 2 adults + 3 children = £600. Add London Travel hotel = £1200. Minus cashback = £1150. QuickFind hotel + London Travel Flights = £1190. Difference = £40

7) What is the cheapest price he can take his family on holiday to Crete for?

b. £1377 - Sun Tours flights for 2 adults + 3 children = £980. Add to Sun Tours hotel = £1530. Minus 10% = £1377

8) If Sun Tours reduced their discount to 5%, what would the difference between the old and new price of taking a holiday to the Algarve be?

d. £65.50 - Sun Tours flights for 2 adults + 3 children = £760. Add to hotel = £1310. 5% of £1310 = £65.50

9) What is the difference in price between Algarve and Barcelona if he books completely through London Travel?

c. £5 - Cost of flights to Algarve = £680. Add to hotel = £1205. Minus £50 = £1155. Cost of flights to Barcelona = £600. Add to hotel = £1200. Minus £50 = £1150. Difference = £5

10) What is the cheapest place he can go to with Sun Tours?

c. Barcelona - Flights for 2 adults + 3 children = £620. Add to hotel = £1220. Minus 10% = £1098

1) Someone wishes to buy 55 plain white Jumpers. How much will this cost?

b. £151.25 - Cost of 55 is £2.75 each. 55 x £2.75 = £151.25

2) A retailer wishes to buy 50 plain white Jumpers and 100 plain coloured Jumpers. How much will this cost?

a. £480 - Cost of 50 plain white jumpers is £3 each, cost of 100 plain coloured jumpers is £3.30 each. 50 x £3 = £150 + (100 x £3.30) = £480

3) Someone wishes to buy 100 plain white Jumpers with black graphics, and 100 plain white Jumpers with coloured graphics. How much will this cost?

e. £810 - Cost of white jumpers with black graphics is 100 x £3.55. Cost of white jumpers with coloured graphics is 100 x £4.55. Total = £850. The discount is eligible on the total order, which was 200 white Jumpers

4) How much profit can a retailer make on 125 coloured Jumpers, if sold at the recommended price?

c. £775 - Cost of coloured Jumpers is 125 x £3.10 = £387.50. Sold at 125 x £9.30 = £1162.50. Difference is £775

5) A retailer buys 60 plain white Jumpers, and 75 coloured Jumpers with black graphics. He sells most of the items, but has 10 white and 15 coloured Jumpers left over. What was the profit/loss?

d. £751.50

Cost of Jumpers is (60 x £2.75) + (75 x £4.80) = £525. Selling 50 plain white + 60 coloured/black graphic Jumpers = (50 x £8.25) + (60 x £14.40) = £1276.50. Difference is £751.50 profit

6) How much will it cost to buy 300 plain coloured jumpers, half with black graphics and half with coloured graphics?

d. £1470 - 300 coloured jumpers cost 300 x £2.90 = £870. Black graphics (150 x £1.50) + Coloured graphics (150 x £2.50) = £600. Total is £1470

7) A shop buys 200 plain white Jumpers, and 100 plain coloured Jumpers. However the shop goes bankrupt, and can only sell them at 1.5x the value they were bought for. What is the difference in profit made compared with if they were sold at 3x the wholesale price.

e. £1245 - Cost of 200 plain white jumpers (200 x £2.50) + 100 plain coloured jumpers (100 x £3.30) = £830. Selling at normal price would result in £830 x 2 profit = £1660. Selling at new price is £830 x 0.5 = £415. Difference is £1245

8) A retailer sells 200 white Jumpers with coloured graphics for a total of £1500 profit. How much must the retailer have been selling each

Jumper for?

a. £10 - Cost of 200 white jumpers Is 200 x £2.50 = £500. £1500 + £500 = £2000, so retailer must have sold total of 200 jumpers for £2000. £2000/200 = £10 each

9) What is the cost of buying 60 plain white Jumpers with coloured graphics, and 80 coloured Jumpers with black graphics?

b. £669 - Cost of 60 white jumpers with coloured graphics = 60 x £4.75 = £285. Cost of 80 coloured jumpers with black graphics = 80 x £4.80 = £384. Total = £669

10) The wholesaler places a 10% discount on all orders. What is the difference between buying 75 plain white Jumpers and 75 coloured Jumpers before, compared with now?

c. £45.37 - Before 75 white jumpers (75 x £2.75) + 75 coloured jumpers (75 x £3.30) costs = £453.75. Now, it costs 10% less = £408.38. Difference = £45.37

QUESTION 3

1) If each length is 25m, how much has Kate swum in total?

c. 87,750 - Total lengths = 700 + 700 + 700 + 700 + 710 = 3510. 3510 x 25m = 87,750m

2) If each length is 25m, how much did the group swim altogether in 2010?

e. 73,500 – Total lengths = 770 + 340 + 550 + 580 + 700 = 2,940. 2940 x 25m = 73,500m

3) If the group raised £15,675 in 2008, and they all charged the same per length, how much were they sponsored per length?

e. £5.50 - Total lengths in 2008 = 750 + 300 + 500 + 600 + 700 = 2,850. 15,675/2,850 = sponsorship per length = £5.50

4) What proportion of the total lengths that year did Katie swim in 2009?

a. 0.18 - Total lengths in 2009 = 760 + 320 + 525 + 580 + 700 = 2885. Katie swam 525, so 525/2885 = 0.18

5) If each length is 25m, what was the average amount swum in 2011?

b. 14,775 - Total lengths in 2011 = 780 + 360 + 575 + 540 + 700 = 2,955. Average = 2955/5 = 591 lengths each. 591 x 25m = 14,775m

6) If they each asked for £6 per length in 2012, how much did they raise in total?

d. £17,820 - Total lengths in 2012 = 790 + 360 + 550 + 560 + 710 = 2970 x £6 = £17,820

7) What was the most anyone swam in the whole 5 year period?

a. Duncan - Duncan swam more than anyone else each year, so it must be him.

8) Who swam the least over 5 years?

b. James - James swam less than anyone else each year, so it must be him

9) What was the percentage change in Duncan's total number of lengths from 2010 to 2012?

d. 2.5% - (790 – 770)/790 = 0.0253...x100 = 2.5%

10) If each length is 25m, how much less did Chris swim in 2010 compared with 2012?

c. 500m - In 2010, Chris swam 25 x 580 = 14,500m. In 2012, Chris swam 25 x 560 = 14,000m. The difference is 500m

QUESTION 4

1) What is the difference in price between three small and two large caricatures?

c.£2 - 3 small ones costs 3 x £10 = £30. 2 large ones cost 2 x £16 = £32. Difference is £2

2) A tourist asks Jayden to draw 5 small caricatures for his children, and 3 large ones for him, his wife, and his brother. How much does this cost the tourist in total?

c. £98 - 5 small ones costs 5 x £10 = £50. 3 large ones cost 3 x £16 = £48. Total is £98

3) Another tourist asks Jayden to draw 4 small caricatures and 4 large ones. He decides to tip her 5%. How much does this cost the tourist in total?

a. £109.20 - 4 small ones costs 4 x £10 = £40. 4 large ones costs 4 x £16 = £64. Total = £104. Add 5% = £109.20

4) Jayden uses £2 worth of material for small caricatures, and £3 for large ones. If she draws 20 small and 15 large caricatures, how much profit does she make?

d. £355 - Its costs her (20 x £2) + (15 x £3) in materials = £85. She receives (20 x £10) + (15 x £16) = £440. Difference is £355.

5) Jayden uses £2 worth of material for small caricatures, and £3 for large ones. If she needs to draw 13 small and 11 large caricatures, how much will the material cost?

e. £59 - Cost of small ones is 13 x £2 = £26. Cost of large ones is 11 x £3 = £33. Total is £59

6) Jayden believes that the day will be busy, so raises her prices by £1 for small and £2 for large caricatures. She expects that she will have to draw 30 small and 20 large ones. How much money will she receive?

b. £690 - From the small ones she will receive 30 x £11 = £330. From the large ones she will receive 20 x £18 = £360. Total is £690.

7) Jayden believes that the day will be busy, so raises her prices by £1 for small and £2 for large caricatures. On average, she draws 20 small and 15 large caricatures per day. However, due to her increased price, she only draws 15 small and 10 large caricatures. What is the difference in profit on an average day compared to today?

e. £95 - Profit due to price change is (15 x £11) + (10 x £18) = £345. Average profit is (20 x £10) + (15 x £16) = £440. Difference is £95

8) Jayden decides to pin some examples on a board. A small caricature is 20cm long by 15cm wide. A large caricature is 40cm by 30cm. If she wishes to pin 3 small ones side by side, how wide a board will she need?

a. 45cm - Each small caricature is 15cm wide, so 15 x 3 = 45cm

9) Jayden decides to pin some examples on a board. A small caricature is 20cm long by 15cm wide. A large caricature is 40cm by 30cm. If

she decides to pin 3 large ones side by side, and 4 small ones underneath side by side, how big will the board need to be?

b. 60 x 90 - Width of 3 large caricatures is 3 x 30cm = 90cm. Length of one large + one small caricature is 20cm + 40cm = 60cm

10) Jayden gives a 20% discount to her first customer, who orders a large caricature. What will the caricature cost the customer?

d. £12.80 - Large caricature costs £16. £16 x 0.8 = £12.80

QUESTION 5

1) What is the cheapest price value of 2750ml of this product?

   c. £42.50 – 500ml is the cheapest, 500 x 5 = 2500ml, £7.50 x 5 = £37.50, 2500ml + 250ml = 2750ml, 250ml = £5, £37.5 + £5 = £42.50

2) Comparing 2 x 250ml bottles to 500ml what is the percentage increase of cost comparing the 250 bottles to the 500ml

   b. 33% - 2 x 250ml = 2 x £5 = £10, Difference in price/Price of 500ml bottle = £2.50/£7.50 = 33.3% which is rounded down to 33%

3) A local drug store offer a 2 for 1 offer on the 250ml bottles, how much would you save if you wanted 2000ml of the shampoo?

   d. £20 – 2000ml, half is for free. 2000ml/2 = 1000ml. 1000ml/250ml = 4, 4 x £5 = £20

4) Another store sells 360 250ml bottles and 120 500ml bottles, what is the ratio of 250ml to 500ml bottles sold in the store?

   c. 3:1 – 250ml bottles: 500ml bottles, 360:120. ÷ both by 120 to get the simplest form, 3:1

QUESTION 6

1) How long does it take him to reach 150mph?

   b. 11.5 seconds – 165mph = 0-60 + 60-100 + 100-150 + 150-165. 3 + 3.5 + 5 = 11.5seconds

2) He accelerates for 8 seconds, what is his speed?

   e. 115mph – 0-60 = 3seconds, 60-100 = 3.5 seconds, 0-100mph = 6.5. What's left over? 8-6.5 = 1.5. The motorcycle accelerates in the 100-150mph range in 10mph per second so 1.5 seconds = 15mph. 100+15 = 115mph

3) The motorcycle is restricted to 130mph , how long will it take before the restrictions kick in? **c. 9.5 seconds** - 130mph = 0-60 + 60-100 + 30mph in the 100-150 range. This equals, 3 + 3.5 + 3 = 9.5 seconds

4) Another motorcycle takes 5 seconds to reach 90mph is it faster than Alex's motorcycle?

   e. Can't tell – We are only given 0-60 and 60-100 times so we do not know.

QUESTION 7

1) Today has been a busy day, he sales 15 Full English breakfast, 21 Cheeseburgers and 10 The Joe's special. How much profit has me made just considering these three items? **a. £167.50**

   - 15 x £4 = £60, 21 x £2.50 = £52.50, 10 x £5.50 = £55

   - £60 + £52.50 + £55 = £167.50

2) The owner sources a new supplier of ingredients that increase his profit of £1 per Full English breakfast, £0.50 per Cheeseburgers and £2 per The Joe's special. What is the percentage increase in profit on average per day? **b. 27%**

   - Average sales = 8 Full English breakfast, 15 Cheeseburgers, 7 The Joe's special.

   - Old profit = 8 x £4 = £32, 15 x £2.50 = £37.50, 7 x £5.50 = £38.50

   - £32 + £37.50 + £38.50 = £108

   - The new profit values = Old + increase, for example for Full English breakfast £4+£1 = £5

   - New profit = 8 x £5 = £40, 15 x £3 = £45, 7 x £7.50 = £52.50

   - £40 + £45 + £52.50 = £137.50

   - Percentage increase = difference in values/ the comparing value x 100

   - £137.50 - £108 / £108 = 29.5/108 = 0.273 x 100 = 27.3%, rounded down to 27%

3) Using the original profit margins. What is the ratio of the profit of Full English breakfast, Cheeseburger compared to The Joe's special on average per day? **d. £32 : £37.50 : £38.50**

 - Old profit = 8 x £4 = £32, 15 x £2.50 = £37.50, 7 x £5.50 = £38.50

 - = £32 : £37.50 : £38.50

4) The café excels under new management, now on average the café sales 20 Full English breakfast what is this increase compared to the previous average? **a. 5:2**

 - 20 : 8 simplifies to 5:2

CHAPTER 5 : ABSTRACT REASONING

ABSTRACT REASONING

*Your interpretation of symbols, your
planing processes and pattern
recognition*

This section is the Abstract Reasoning practice question, we recommend you refresh your memory on how to approach this section on pages 28 - 45

What is expected of you?

This part of the subtest assesses your ability to identify patterns among abstract shapes that are placed with several insignificant and distracting shapes. The latter exist to confuse you and could potentially lead you to draw incorrect conclusions. This subtest tests your lateral thinking ability and requires you to evaluate and think about the options critically. You need to be able to quickly identify patterns, rules and trends in a given set of data, and then apply this information to solve the question in front of you.

Candidates have 14 minutes in which 55 questions associated with sets of shapes need to be answered. There are four different item types in the UKCAT (according to the official UKCAT guide 2013) and candidates may see one or two of these item types.

For type 1, you will be presented with two sets of shapes labelled "Set A" and "Set B". You will be given a test shape and asked to decide whether the test shape belongs to Set A, Set B, or Neither.

For type 2, you will be presented with a series of shapes. You will be asked to select the next shape in the series.

When you look at each question, ask yourself,

'What is consistent? '
'What information can I eliminate? '
'What is the difference between the shapes in set A to those in set B?'
'What makes this particular shape stand out from the rest? '

Top tips!

1. Don't rush the answer. Look carefully at both sets A and B before trying to identify what the common theme/rule is

2. Don't simply consider each shape within a set, but try and look at an entire set and see what it has to offer (e.g. count the sides of all the shapes in Set A, rather than each shape)

3. Identify the relationship of each shape to the others in a given box for each set and remember there may be more than one rule

4. Simply flag items that you get stuck on, and come back to them at the end of the section, or else you will waste valuable time

5. Use your whiteboard to quickly note down the aspects that you can use as a checklist for each question, e.g. sides, number of shape, colour etc

Abstract Reasoning Questions

Judging from past exams approximately 90% of your answers might be in this format

Question 1 - Which set does it belong to? A, B or Niether?

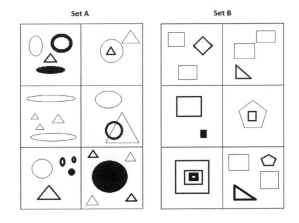

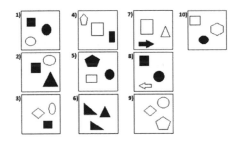

Question 2 - Which set does it belong to? A, B or Niether?

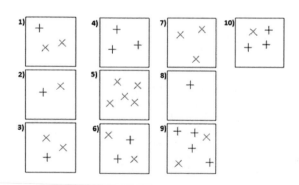

Question 3 - Which set does it belong to? A, B or Niether?

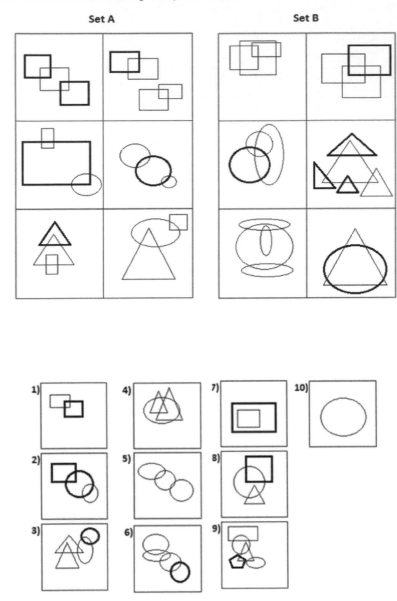

Question 4 - Which set does it belong to? A, B or Niether?

Set A   Set B

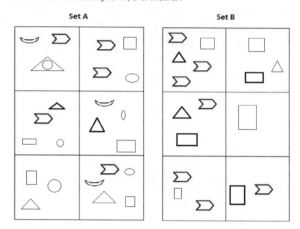

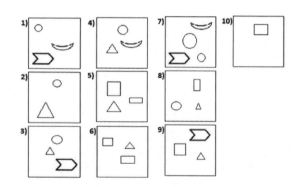

93

Question 5 - Which set does it belong to? A, B or Niether?

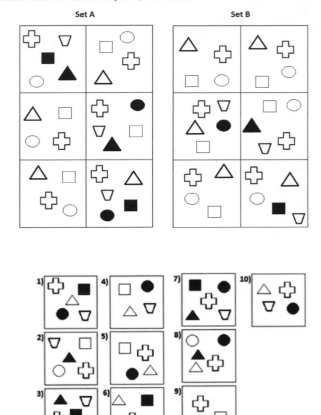

Question 6 - Which set does it belong to? A, B or Niether?

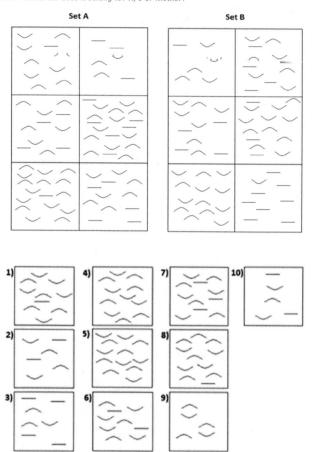

Judging from past exams approximately 10%of your answers might be in this format

Question 7 - Which box completes the series?

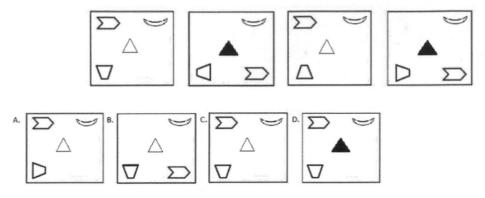

Question 8 - Which box completes the series?

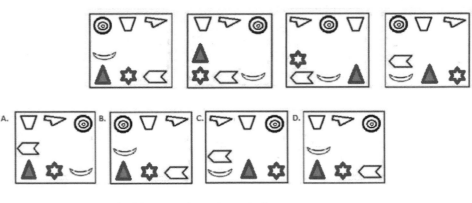

Question 9- Which box completes the series?

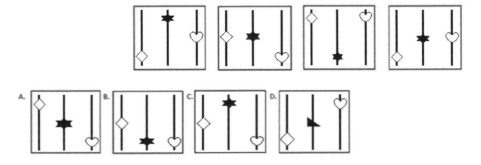

Question 10 - Which box completes the series?

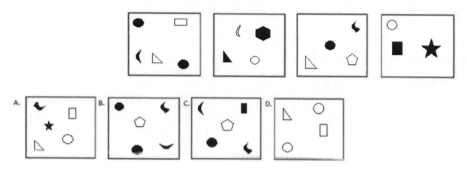

Abstract reasoning Answers

Question 1

Rule: Set A has at least one circle and one triangle, and no other shapes. Set B has only straight sided shapes.

Answers

1) **Neither** – has a four-sided shape and has a circle

2) **Neither** - has a four-sided shape and has a circle

3) **Neither** - has a four-sided shape and has a circle

4) **B** – has only straight sided shapes

5) **Neither** - has a four-sided shape and has a circle

6) **B** – has only straight sided shapes

7) **B** – has only straight sided shapes

8) **Neither** - has a four-sided shape and has a circle

9) **Neither** - has a four-sided shape and has a circle

10) **Neither** - has a four-sided shape and has a circle

Question 2

Rule: Set A has an even number of '+'s. Set B has an odd number of 'x's.

Answers

1) **Neither** – odd number of '+' and even number of 'x's

2) **B** - odd number of 'x'

3) **Neither** – odd number of '+' and even number of 'x's

4) **Neither** – odd number of '+' no 'x'

5) **B** - odd number of 'x's

6) **A** – even number of '+'s and even number of 'x's but this doesn't matter

7) **B** - odd number of 'x'

8) **Neither** - odd number of 'x'

9) **A** - even number of '+'s and even number of 'x's but this doesn't matter

10) **B** - odd number of '+' and odd number of 'x's but this doesn't matter

Question 3

Rule: Both use only a mixture of circles, triangles and four sided shape. Set A has two intersections, Set B has four intersections.

Answers

1) **Neither** – has one intersection

2) **A** – has two intersection

3) **Neither** - has three intersections

4) **Neither** - has five intersections

5) **A** – has two intersection

6) **Neither** - has three intersections

7) **Neither** - has no intersection

8) **A** - has two intersection

9) **Neither** - has four intersections but uses a five sided shape

10) **Neither** - has no intersection

Question 4

Rule: Set A has one circle. Set B has no curved edges.

Answers

1) **A** - has one circle

2) **A** - has one circle

3) **A** - has one circle

4) **A** - has one circle

5) **B** - has no curved edges.

6) **B** - has no curved edges.

7) **Neither** -- has two circles

8) **A** - has one circle

9) **B** - has no curved edges.

10) **B** - has no curved edges.

Question 5

Rule: Both have 4 shapes, Set A has a 5th quadrilateral if two are shaded. Set B has a 5th quadrilateral if one is shaded.

Answers

1) **A** – Has four shapers and a 5th four sided shape if because there are two shaded

2) **B** – Has four shapers and a 5th four sided shape if because there is one shaded

3) **A** – Has four shapers and a 5th four sided shape if because there are two shaded

4) **Neither** – Has four shapes but not a 5th one even though on is shaded

5) **B** – Has four shapers and a 5th four sided shape if because there is one shaded

6) **Neither** – Has four shapes but not a 5th one even though on is shaded

7) **Neither** – Has only three shapes

8) **Neither** - Has four shapers, two shaded and has 5th shape but it is not a four-sided shape

9) **Neither** – Has only three shapes

10) **Neither** – Has four shapes but not a 5th one even though on is shaded

Question 6

Rule: Set A has one more peak than trough, and at least one horizontal line. Set B has one less peak than trough.

Answers

1) **B** - has one less peak than trough.

2) **Neither** – has the same number of peaks and troughs

3) **A** - has one more peak than trough, and at least one horizontal line

4) **Neither**- has one more peak than trough, but no horizontal line

5) **Neither** – has the same number of peaks and troughs

6) **B** - has one less peak than trough.

7) **Neither** – has the same number of peaks and troughs

8) **A** - has one more peak than trough, and at least one horizontal line

9) **Neither** - - has one more peak than trough, but no horizontal line

10) **B** - has one less peak than trough.

Question 7

c. – First thing to take note of is that none of the shapes are changing. The triangle at the centre is changing shade consistently, On and off. In step four the triangle is shaded so it should be unshaded in the completing box. What are the other shapes doing? The crescent shape, Seems to be constantly there are, without any change at the top right hand corner for all four steps of the series so it's safe to presume that it should be present in the bow that completes the series. The trapezium shape, is at that set postion in the bottom left corner but it rotates 90° clockwise in each step regardless of the shade of the triangle. The completing box the trapezium should be on the bottom left corner rotated 90° clockwise from step four. Last but not least the arrow shape is at two positions the top left and the bottom right corner, does the postion change in relation to any other shapes? Yes it does, if the triangle is shaded the arrow is in the bottom right and if unshaded, top left.

Question 8

d. – Similar to the question before the shapes are not changing. The spaces which the shapes occupy are the same, the three in a straight line at the top and an elongated L-configuration at the bottom however, the positions seem to change from step to step. If we look closely the top three shapes move along right to left, while bottom four are moving in a clockwise fashion along the L-shape. The completing box should be the continuation of these movements from step four

Question 9

c. – At first glance you can see there are three lines and three different shapes on these lines, the shapes do not change. They move positions in a fashion that appears to be moving on the lines, but they do know move in the same manner. If you look at each shape individually you can see that the first diamond shape moves up the line. In step 3 – 4, where it reaches the top, it starts again from the bottom. Second shape, the shaded star ✦ , moves down the line however in step 3-4 when it reaches the bottom, it starts moving up the line like if it was bouncing off the bottom line. The heart shape starts in the midpoint of the line and like the shaded star moved down the line. However in step 2 -3 when the shape reaches the bottom line like it was the opposite of the diamond shape but under the same rules, it starts again from top. The answer is the continuation of these movements on the line from step four.

Question 10

b. – At first glance you might be overwhelmed by the lack of obvious structure, shapes, spaces, positions, quantity of shapes changing inconsistently. You can spend a lot of time trying to make sense of chaos. A key thing to do is to focus on what is consistent not what is inconsistent. This is a takes practice. The one obvious consistent aspect is that there are always shaded shapes in the boxes. We've eliminated the effect of other shapes due their inconsistently. Most students get stuck at this point, but if you recall from the breakdown sections, a good way to break it down is look at two steps individually. I f you take steps 1 and 2 one thing you might notice is the shapes that are shaded, in step 1 the circles are shaded but in the 2nd step it isn't. What's going on? If you then look for the circle in step 3 it changes back to shaded, there must be a link, what is it? What does a circle have in common with the other shapes? If you look overall at step 1 again, the shapes that are shaded in are not just circles but shapes without clear defined lines. What happens to these shapes in step 2? Ah ha, the pattern emerges, the shading alternates from shaded circle shapes to shaded straight lined shapes and so

on. In step 4 the shaded shapes are shapes with clear defined lines so the completing box will be of circles and shapes without clearly defined lines. This is a difficult question, do not worry if you didn't get it the first time, the key is to learn and build up from your mistakes and use the steps given to you in the breakdown section

DECISION ANALYSIS

Your ability to categorise and cluster information. To test your ability to switch between categories.

This section is the Decision Analysis practice question, we recommend you refresh your memory on how to approach this section on pages 15 - 19.

What is expected of you?

This part encompasses 28 questions. Although this section has the least amount of questions in comparison to the other parts of the test, the recommended time to be spent on this part is 34 minutes (the longest out of all five). This implies that you SHOULD NOT rush your answers but instead consider the codes carefully and manipulate the information on the screen.

There is an associated confidence rating for each item, which is simply a score (a 5 point scale, 1 being the least confident and 5 being the most) of how confident you feel about the answer that you have provided. It is simply a measure of how aware you are of your decisions. It is best to answer these honestly and candidates should not waste time thinking about how sure they are. These scores in conjunction with your decision analysis scores are to gauge the awareness of your decisions. However, the confidence ratings will NOT contribute to your overall score and will not be passed onto your Universities of Choice.

The codes will evidently get more complicated as you go along, so it is advisable to use your whiteboard to make better sense of the harder codes. Remember to answer each question in full or else the test won't let you proceed to the next stage.

If you recall from the breakdown, the questions will ask you one of the following :

- The best interpretation of the coded message - Judging from past exams approximately 50% of your answers might be in this format.
- Which codes would be the most useful addition to deliver a certain message and which two words would be useful in coding a sentence - Judging from past exams approximately 50%of your answers might be in these formats.

Top tips!!

1. We suggest that you don't waste time reading all of the codes at the start and instead start with the codes relevant to each question-this will maximise your efficiency in this subtest
2. Write out the code literally as it is in the question FIRST
3. Eliminate options which do not satisfy the components of the code
4. Use your judgement to analyze the code, the answer is not always a literal translation (for example, a code that reads *noble (opposite man)* could refer to a countess, noble(brave,man) could refer to a knight etc.
5. When practicing, we recommend doing ten questions (of one code box) at a time and then checking your answers, so that things are still fresh in your mind and you understand the meanings better.

Decision Analysis Questions

Question 1

A = Outside	1 = House	! = Soft
B = Inside	2 = Window	@ = Hard
C = Top	3 = Door	£ = Old
D = Bottom	4 = Cave	$ = New
E = Many	5 = Hut	% = Shiny
F = Exchange	6 = Jewellery	^ = Dull
G = Break	7 = Food	& = Weak
H = Past	8 = Robber	* = Cold
J = Next	9 = Wall	
K = Buy	10 = Money	
L = Give	11 = Cover	
M = Contain	12 = Sun	
N = Increase	13 = Rain	
	14 = Wind	
	15 = Bug	
	16 = Bed	

1) What is the best interpretation of the following coded message? 1, M, 2(C,11)

The house has a ceiling

The house has a roof

The window was on the ceiling

The wall has a window

The house has a roof window

2) What is the best interpretation of the following coded message? 5, (E, 9), !
The walls were soft

The soft walls made the hut

The hut walls are soft

The wall of the hut is soft

The wall is soft

3) What is the best interpretation of the following coded message? 8, F, 6, 10

The robber stole jewellery and money

The robber stole jewellery instead of money

The robber stole money instead of jewellery

The robber swapped the jewellery for money

4) What is the best interpretation of the following coded message? (2, 11), H, £

The curtain covered the window

The window was covered by a curtain

The curtains were old

The curtain was old

The window was covered

5) What is the best interpretation of the following coded message? 4, (*,N), 5

The cave was very cold

The cave was colder than the hut

The hut was very cold

The caves were colder than the hut

The caves and huts were cold

6) What is the best interpretation of the following coded message? G(C,9), L, 13, B

The rain broke the ceiling

The ceiling was raining

The broken ceiling let rain in

The ceiling broke

The rain came from the ceiling

(D, 9, 11), !

11(D,9), !

(D, 11), !

D, 9, 11, N!

7) What is the best interpretation of the following coded message? 8, G, 2, B

(9, 11), !

11) What would the best way to encode the following message be? The thief bought cold food

The robber stole the window

The robber entered via the window

The robber tried to break the window

The window broke

The robber took the window

8, (J,K), (*,7);

8, (H,F), (*,7)

8, F, *,7

8, K, *,7

8, (H,K), *,7

8) What is the best interpretation of the following coded message? A, *, 13

12) What would the best way to encode the following message be? The huts broke in the storm

The rain was colder outside

It was cold and rainy

Rain is cold

Outside the house, it was cold and rainy;

Outside, it was cold and rainy

E, 5, (N, 13, 14)

N (13, 14), G, 5

N (13, 14), G, E

(N, 13, 14), G, (E,5)

5, G, (N, 13, 14)

9) What is the best interpretation of the following coded message? 8, F, 7, 10

13) What would the best way to encode the following message be? There were bugs in the duvet

The robber stole money for food

The robber bought food with money

The robber stole food and money

The robber ate food with stolen money

The robber needed money and food

(16, 11), (H,M), 15

16, 11, (M,15)

16, (H,M), 15

(16, 11), M, 15

16, M, 15

10) What would the best way to encode the following message be? The carpet is soft

14) What would the best way to encode the following message be? The robber broke the weak door

8, H, G, &3

8, G, &3

8, (H,G), &3

8, G, 3

&3, G, 8

15) What would the best way to encode the following message be? The new coins are shiny

E, $, @, 10, %

(E, 10), %;

£, E(@,10),%

@, E(%,10), %

E($, 10), %

16) What would the best way to encode the following message be? The old wallpaper had cracks

£(9, 11), M, EG

£(9, 11), H, G

(£,9), (E,G)

£(9, 11), (H,M), (E+G)

9£, M, G

17) What would the best way to encode the following message be? The hut used to be a house

5, H, 1

(5,H), 1

5, (H,1)

1, (5,H)

(1,H), 5

18) What would the best way to encode the following message be? The cave was cold

4, H, *

4, M,(H, *)

4, (M,H), (B, *)

4, (H,M), (N,*)

4, (H,M), *

19) Which two options would be the most useful additions to the codes in the table above, in order to convey the following message accurately? The robber fell to the floor of the bungalow

Floor

Fall

Of

Bungalow

The

20) Which two options would be the most useful additions to the codes in the table above, in order to convey the following message accurately? The robber ate hot food

Eat

The

Hot

Single

Meal

105

21) Which two options would be the most useful additions to the codes in the table above, in order to convey the following message accurately? The bed bugs climbed to middle of the ceiling

To

Ceiling

Middle

The

Climb

22) Which two options would be the most useful additions to the codes in the table above, in order to convey the following message accurately? The tree-house gave protection from the storm

Tree

Protection

Storm

Gave

Tree-house

23) Which two options would be the most useful additions to the codes in the table above, in order to convey the following message accurately? The roof-window is being polished so it is glossy

Getting

Polished

Glossy

Roof

Is

24) Which two options would be the most useful additions to the codes in the table above, in order to convey the following message accurately? The wasp could not see the ceiling

Ceiling

Yellow

No

Stinging

Blind

25) Which two options would be the most useful additions to the codes in order to convey the following message accurately? The wallpaper is gloomy and cracked

Paper

Cracked

And

Gloomy

The

26) Which two options would be the most useful additions to the codes in order to convey the following message accurately? The robber exchanged coins for diamonds

Small

Metal

Shiny

Diamonds

Clear

A = Opposite	1 = Vehicle	! = Slow
B = Other	2 = Fly	@ = Fast
C = Keen	3 = Water	£ = Old
D = Increase	4 = Road	$ = Happy
E = Future	5 = Wheel	% = Bad
F = People	6 = Run	^ = Fat
G = Lots	7 = Female	& = Big
H = Single	8 = Fall	
J = More	9 = Crash	
K = None	10 = Race	
L = Less	11 = Time	
	12 = Television	
	13 = Hair	
	14 = Health	
	15 = Post	
	16 = Cargo	

1) What is the best interpretation of the following coded message? (A,7), 6(A,E),10

She ran a race

She is running a race

He ran a race

She drove in a race

His race was run

2) What is the best interpretation of the following coded message? F(A,^), C, (14, 6)

Thin people like exercise

Thin people like to run

Thin people have good health

Fat people like to run

Healthy people are thin

3) What is the best interpretation of the following coded message? !(1, 4), 9, K

The slow car did not crash

Slow cars do not crash

The car did not crash as it was slow

The vehicle did not crash

The slow car crashed

4) What is the best interpretation of the following coded message? (1, 2), (J,@), (1, 3)

Planes beat boats

Fast boats are like planes

The fast plane landed on water

The plane quickly became a boat

Planes are faster than boats

5) What is the best interpretation of the following coded message? (7,G),(8,A)

The women are jumping

The women jumped

They jumped

They fall

The women didn't fall

6) What is the best interpretation of the following coded message? (7, 15), (A,E), H

The woman received one item of post

The woman posted one letter

The post was feminine

The postwoman was alone

The postwomen were single

7) What is the best interpretation of the following coded message? (4, 6), (A,E), (D,@)

The roadrunner was very fast

The road was run very fast

The race was fast

The roadrunner was fast

The road was run fast

8) What is the best interpretation of the following coded message? (F, K), 10, 9

No one crashed

No one in the race crashed

People crashed in the race

There was a crash in the race

There were no collisions in the race

9) What is the best interpretation of the following coded message? (&, 10), !

The marathon was slow

The race is slowly getting bigger

The race is bigger

The big race was slow

The marathon is slow

10) What would the best way to encode the following message be? The television will be old

12, £

12, E, &

12, AE, &

12, E, £

12, (11, E)

11) What would the best way to encode the following message be? Lorries are slower than cars

1&, 4, (D,!), (1, 4)

& (1, 4), (D,!), (1,4)

&(1, 4), !, (1, 4)

&(1, 4,16), D(A,^), (1, 4)

&(1, 4), A^, (1, 4)

12) What would the best way to encode the following message be? The old women liked water exercises

£(G, 7), (A,E), (3, 14)

(£,G, 7), C, (3, 14)

(7, £), A,E,C, (3, 14)

£(G, 7), C(A,E), 3(6, 14)

(£,7), C, (3, 14)

13) What would the best way to encode the following message be? He is obese

(A,7), (D,&)

A,7, G,&

7, (D,^)

Λ, (&,7)

(A,7), G (D,^)

14) What would the best way to encode the following message be? More women run than men

D(7,G), (D,A), A(G,7), 6

(G,7), 6, A(G,7)

(J, 7), 6, A(7, G)

J(G,7), 6, A(7,G)

L7, (AD, AG7), (14, 6)

15) What would the best way to encode the following message be? Women have longer hair than men

7, J(^, 13), A(G,7)

(G,7), (J,13), (A,7)

7(G, 7), &(J,13), G, 7

7, (J, 13), (A,7)

(G,7), J(&, 13), A(G,7)

16) What would the best way to encode the following message be? The television will be old

12, 11, £

12, E, (D,£)

12, 11, (D,£)

12, E, £

12, £

17) What would the best way to encode the following message be? The boat is sinking

(1, 3), 8

(1, 3), (8, 3)

(1, 3), 9, (8, 3)

3, (8, 3)

(1, 3), (E8, 3)

18) Which two options would be the most useful additions to the codes in order to convey the following message accurately? The post was delivered late due to a car crash

Car

Past

After

Given

Was

19) Which two options would be the most useful additions to the codes in order to convey the following message accurately? Women drive quicker than men

Quick

Drive

Quicker

Compare

Man

20) Which two options would be the most useful additions to the codes in order to convey the following message accurately? Time will tell the winner of the sprint

Sprint

Result

Will

Present

Winner

Sea

From

Into

21) Which two options would be the most useful additions to the codes in order to convey the following message accurately? Her hair is blonde, thick and shiny

Blonde

Thick

Her

Shiny

And

22) Which two options would be the most useful additions to the codes in order to convey the following message accurately? The wheels on the bus go round and round

Round

Repeat

Wheels

Bus

Go

23) Which two options would be the most useful additions to the codes in order to convey the following message accurately? The cargo plane fell from the sky into the sea

Plane

Sky

24) Which two options would be the most useful additions to the codes in order to convey the following message accurately? The journey was longer than planned

Longer

Long

Plan

Compare

Journey

25) Which two options would be the most useful additions to the codes in order to convey the following message accurately? People crashed on the road due to holes

Holes

On

The

Because

Car

26) Which two options would be the most useful additions to the codes in order to convey the following message accurately? My big, fat, broadcast wedding

Broadcast

Personal

Wedding

Male

Marriage

Question 3

A = Opposite	1 = Treasure	! = Wet
B = Many	2 = Pyramid	@ = Hot
C = Personal	3 = Sand	£ = Search
D = Trust	4 = Sun	$ = Quick
E = Extreme	5 = Water	% = Small
F = Take	6 = Vegetation	^ = Reliable
G = Generalise	7 = Camel	& = Stop
H = Reverse	8 = Horse	
J = Single	9 = Storm	
K = Always	10 = Salt	
L = Similar	11 = Food	
	12 = People	
	13 = Caravan	
	14 = Seat	
	15 = Leader	
	16 = War	

1) What is the best interpretation of the following coded message? 9, (A,F), 6, 5

The storm led to an oasis

The vegetation was wet after the storm

The storm made the vegetation wet

The vegetation needed water from the storm

The storm gave water to the vegetation

2) What is the best interpretation of the following coded message? 12, (K, D), 15

The leader needed the trust of the people

The people held trust in their leader

The people always trust their leader

The people trusted the leader

The people always trusted the leader

3) What is the best interpretation of the following coded message? 15, (K, £), 1

The leader was on the lookout for treasure

The leader always looked for treasure

The leader found the treasure

The leader always looked for his treasure

The leader looked after the treasure

4) What is the best interpretation of the following coded message? 9 (A,$), &, 16

The storm stopped the war

War broke out during the storm

The storm stopped with the war

The war stopped with the storm

The long storm halted the war

5) What is the best interpretation of the following coded message? (13, &), (5, 6), 3

The caravan reached an oasis in the desert

The caravan reached water in the desert

There was vegetation in the sand

The caravan stopped in the sand

They reached water and vegetation

6) What is the best interpretation of the following coded message? C,15, K(F, 12), 2(A,J)

The leader always showed the people to the pyramids

The leader always found the pyramids

My leader always reached the pyramids

My leader always led the people to the pyramids

The people sent the leader to the pyramids

7) What is the best interpretation of the following coded message? 7, 8, L

Camels are different to horses

Camels are different; Horses are different

Camels and horses are not different

Camels and horses get along

8) What is the best interpretation of the following coded message? (J,12), 14, 8

He sat on a horse

The person sat on a horse

They sat the horse down

The person made the horse sit

The person sat on a camel

9) What would the best way to encode the following message be? My horse drinks water

(C,8), (F, 10)

C,8, F, 10

(C,8), F, 5

(C,8), (11, 10)

C8, 11, 10

10) What would the best way to encode the following message be? The diamond is tiny

%, E%

(1,E), (E,%)

(4, 1), %

1, (E,%)

1, %

11) What would the best way to encode the following message be? The desert has a drought

3, E(A,!)

(E,3), (H,5)

3, (A, 5)

(E,3), (A,5)

3, (EA, !)

12) What would the best way to encode the following message be? The people trust their camels

12, D, (C,7)

12, D, (A,J), (C,7)

12, D, (A,J), 7

12, D, 7

7, D, 12

13) What would the best way to encode the following message be? The leader trusts his horse

15, D, (A,J), (C,8)

15, D, 8

15, D, (C,8)

15, (D, 8)

(C,15), D,(C, 8)

@, (5, 6)

(%, @), (5, 6)

@(A,E), (5, 6)

(%, @), 6

14) What would the best way to encode the following message be? The search for treasure leads to war

(£, 1), (F, 16)

£, 1, (A,Γ), 16

(£, 1), G, 16

£, 1, K, (A,F), 16

(£, 1), 16

18) What would the best way to encode the following message be? One small group takes the treasure

(%,12), F, 1

(J,12), F, 1

C(%,12), F, 1

J(%,12), F, 1

J, 12, F, 1

15) What would the best way to encode the following message be? The horse sits on the desert

8, (G,14), 3

8, 14, 3

8, A(14, 3)

(8, 14), 3

(G,8), 14, 3

19) What would the best way to encode the following message be? The food is very salty

11, 10

(G,11), 10

11, (G,10)

11, (E,10)

11, (A,10)

16) What would the best way to encode the following message be? The great storm quickly cleared up

(A, 9), (&, $)

(A, 9), H

(E,9), &

9(A,%), &, $

(E,9), H

20) Which two options would be the most useful additions to the codes in the table above, in order to convey the following message accurately? Horses are more reliable than camels

More

Compare

Many

Plural

Better

17) What would the best way to encode the following message be? Warm oasis

@(A,E), 3(5, 6)

21) Which two options would be the most useful additions to the codes in the table above, in order to convey the following message accurately? He was the leader of the group

Group

Male

Past

Once

Them

22) Which two options would be the most useful additions to the codes in the table above, in order to convey the following message accurately? The child is the leader in the quest for treasure and fame

Quest

Fame

Present

Baby

Adult

23) Which two options would be the most useful additions to the codes in the table above, in order to convey the following message accurately? The sun heated the sand

Make

The

Past

Ground

Shone

24) Which two options would be the most useful additions to the codes in the table above, in order to convey the following message accurately? In the desert, storms are long

Storms

Long

Are

Contain

Desert

25) Which two options would be the most useful additions to the codes in the table above, in order to convey the following message accurately? The leader must be strong and reliable

Strong

And

He

Must

Leader

26) Which two options would be the most useful additions to the codes in the table above, in order to convey the following message accurately? The vegetation needs water to grow

To

Wants

Require

Liquid

Grow

Decision Analysis Answers

Question 1

A = Outside	1 = House	! = Soft
B = Inside	2 = Window	@ = Hard
C = Top	3 = Door	£ = Old
D = Bottom	4 = Cave	$ = New
E = Many	5 = Hut	% = Shiny
F = Exchange	6 = Jewellery	^ = Dull
G = Break	7 = Food	& = Weak
H = Past	8 = Robber	* = Cold
J = Next	9 = Wall	
K = Buy	10 = Money	
L = Give	11 = Cover	
M = Contain	12 = Sun	
N = Increase	13 = Rain	
	14 = Wind	
	15 = Bug	
	16 = Bed	

1) **The house has a roof window**
   M means contain, or has. 2(C,11) literally means window of the top cover, which in this context it best translates to roof window.

2) **The hut walls are soft**
   (E, 9) is many wall, or walls. There is no past tense.

3) **The robber swapped the jewellery for money**
   F, meaning exchange, best translates to swap rather than stole.

4) **The curtain was old**
   (2, 11) means window cover, which means curtain. H is past, so in the past (ie was). There is no plural.

5) **The cave was colder than the hut**
   (*,N) means increase cold literally, which is likely to mean colder. Cave comes before hut in the code, so the cave was colder than the hut.

6) **The broken ceiling let rain in**
   G(C,9) means break in top, this best translates to broken ceiling. Give can mean let, and B in.

7) **The robber entered via the window**
   Literally, this code means Robber, Break, Window, Inside. There is no reference to stole, try, the past tense, or take. The coupling

of break and inside in the same sentence refers to 'break in', or enter.

8) **Outside, it was cold and rainy**
   *, 13 probably means cold and rainy rather than cold rain. A means outside. There is no reference to house.

9) **The robber bought food with money**
   F, or exchange, more likely means bought than stole, ate or need.

10) **11(D, 9),! –** Cover of (bottom + wall), soft
11) **8, (H, K),*,7 –** Robber, (past + buy), cold, food
12) **N(13, 14), G, (E, 5) –** Increase(rain + wind), break, (many + hut)
13) **(16, 11), (H, M), 15 –** (bed + cover), (past + contain), bugs
14) **8,(H, G), &, 3 –** Robber, (past + break), weak, door
15) **$, E(@, 10), % -** New, many(hard + money), shiny
16) **£(9, 11), (H, M), (E, G) –** Old(wall + cover), (past + contain), (many + cracks)
17) **5, H, 1 –** Hut, past, house
18) **4, (H, M), * -** Cave,(past + contain), cold

19) **Fall**
    Bungalow

    Bottom Wall could mean floor. Of and The are not necessary in codes generally.

20) **Hot**
    Eat

    The is not necessary in codes generally. There is no reference to single or meal (food is already coded).

21) **Climb**
    To

    Ceiling can be coded for by top inside wall. Bug is already a code. There is nothing to replace climb, or to. The is not necessary in codes generally.

22) **Tree**
    Protection

    Increase Rain Wind can be used for storm. Give is already a code. House is already a code.

23) **Getting**
    Polished

    Glossy can be coded for by shiny. Outside Top Wall can be used for Roof. Is not necessary in codes generally. Getting replaces is being in the message.

24) **Stinging**
    Blind

    Ceiling can be coded for by Inside Top Wall. No isn't a useful replacement for not. Yellow would not help describe the wasp as Stinging when used in conjunction with bug. Blind can replace 'could not see'

25) **Gloomy**
    Paper

Cracked can be coded for by break. And can be replaced using correct grammar (eg brackets). The is not necessary in codes generally.

26) Metal
Diamonds

Metal can be used in conjunction with money to code for coins. Small, shiny and clear would not help describe anything in the message.

Question 2

A = Opposite	1 = Vehicle	! = Slow
B = Other	2 = Fly	@ = Fast
C = Keen	3 = Water	£ = Old
D = Increase	4 = Road	$ = Happy
E = Future	5 = Wheel	% = Bad
F = People	6 = Run	^ = Fat
G = Lots	7 = Female	& = Big
H = Single	8 = Fall	
J = More	9 = Crash	
K = None	10 = Race	
L = Less	11 = Time	
	12 = Television	
	13 = Hair	
	14 = Health	
	15 = Post	
	16 = Cargo	

1) **He ran a race**
   (A, 7) means male, so not she. 6(A, E) means past of run, so it is in the past tense (ran).

2) **Thin people like exercise**
   (A, ^) is thin. F(A, ^) is thin people, C, Keen, can mean like. (14, 16) Health Run is more likely to mean exercise than simply run.

3) **The slow car did not crash**
   (1, 4)! Literally means slow road vehicle, or slow car. None, Crash would mean no crash, or did not crash. There is no plural in the code.

4) **Planes are faster than boats**
   The code means planes, more fast, boats. The best version of this is planes are faster than boats.

5) **The women are jumping**
   (8, A) more likely means jump than fall. There is no past tense in the code.

6) **The post woman was alone**
   (7, 15), or post, female means post woman.

7) **The roadrunner was very fast**
   The code for run is not related to the past tense in the message. There is no reference to race. (4, 6) is coupled in brackets so means roadrunner.

8) **No one in the race crashed**
   (F, K) means no one. 10 refers to race.

9) **The marathon is slow**
   Big race is another way to say marathon. There is no past tense.

10) **12, E, £ - Television, future, old**

11) **&(1, 4, 16), (D, !), (1, 4) – Big (vehicle, road, cargo), (increase, slow), (vehicle, road)**

12) **£(7, G), C(A, E), 3(6, 14) – Old (many + female), keen (opposite + future), water (health + run)**

13) **(A,7), G(D, ^) – (Opposite + female) , lots(increase + fat)**

14) **J(7, G), 6, A(7, G) – More (female + lots), run, opposite(female + lots)**

15) **(G, 7), J(&, 13), A(G, 7) – (Lots + female), more(big + hair), opposite(Lots + female)**

16) **12, E, £ - Television, future, old**

17) **(1, 3), (8, 3) – (Vehicle + water), (fall + water)**

18) **Given**
    After

    Car can be coded for by road vehicle. Past can be coded for by opposite future. Was is past tense, so can also be coded for by opposite future. Given can replace delivered. After can replace due to.

19) **Drive**
    Compare

    Quick and quicker can be replaced by fast and more fast. Man can be coded for by opposite female.

20) **Winner**
    Result

    Fast race can code for sprint. Will is not necessary to make the message make sense in code. Present is not in the message.

21) **Blonde**
    Shiny

    Fat can code for thick. Her could be written as female. And is not necessary if brackets are used.

22) **Round**
    Wheels

    Repeat is not necessary if we have Round and And. Bus can be coded for by big people road vehicle.

23) **Sky**
    Sea

    Plane can be coded for by fly vehicle. Sky and Sea are more important as the code would be decipherable without from and into. Water could be used as sea, but, it could mean river, lake et cetera. It's too vague

24) **Journey**
    Plan

Long and Longer can be coded for by more and time. Compare is not in the message.

25) Holes
    Because

On and The are not necessary for codes in general. Car can be communicated with road vehicle.

26) **Personal**
    Wedding

Broadcast can be coded for by television. Male can be written as opposite female. Wedding is better than marriage as it is like for like.

Question 3

A = Opposite	1 = Treasure	! = Wet
B = Many	2 = Pyramid	@ = Hot
C = Personal	3 = Sand	£ = Search
D = Trust	4 = Sun	$ = Quick
E = Extreme	5 = Water	% = Small
F = Take	6 = Vegetation	^ = Reliable
G = Generalise	7 = Camel	& = Stop
H = Reverse	8 = Horse	
J = Single	9 = Storm	
K = Always	10 = Salt	
L = Similar	11 = Food	
	12 = People	
	13 = Caravan	
	14 = Seat	
	15 = Leader	
	16 = War	

1) **The storm gave water to the vegetation**
   (A,F) means give. Water and vegetation have not been linked together, so oasis is not a good translation.

2) **The people always trust their leader**
   (K, D) means always trust. 15 means personal leader, which in this context can be translated to their leader. There is no code for held. There is no past tense.

3) **The leader always looked for treasure**
   (K, £) means always search, or always look(ed). There is no personal reference, so not his treasure.

4) **The long storm halted the war**
   (A,$) can translate to long. & means stop, or halt.

5) **The caravan reached an oasis in the desert**
   (13, &) means caravan stopped, or reached. (5, 6) can mean oasis due to the brackets linking the two words. 3 means sand, which can be extended to desert.

6) **My leader always led the people to the pyramids**
   (c, 15) Personal leader means my leader. K(F, 12) means always take people, but can also mean always lead when people is added. (A, J) means plural.

7) **Camels and horses are not different**
   (7, 8) means camels and horse as they are linked. L means similar, or not different.

8) **The person sat on a horse**
   J12 translates to single people, or person. 14 means seat, but as there are no other viable options with seat, we must assume it means sat.

9) **(C, 8), F, 5 – (Perosnal + horse), takes, water**
10) **1, (E, %) – Treasure, (extreme + small)**
11) **(E,3), (A, 5) – (extreme + sand), (opposite + water)**
12) **12, D, (C, 7) – People, trust, (personal + camel)**
13) **15, D, (C, 8) – Leader, trust, (personal + horse)**
14) **£, 1, (A, F), 16 – Search, treasure, (opposite + take), war**
15) **8, 14, 3 – Horse, seat, dessert**
16) **9(A, %), &, $ - Storm(opposite + small), stop, quick**
17) **@(A, E), 3(5, 6) – Hot(Opposite + extreme), sand(water + vegataion)**
18) **J(%, 12), F, 1 – Single(Small + People), take, treasure**
19) **11, (E,10) – Food, (Extreme + salt)**

20) **More**
    Compare

Many can be coded for by opposite single. Plural can be coded for by the same. Better is not in the message. Compare codes for them.

21) **Male**
    Past

People can replace group, them is not an ideal replacement for group. Future can join reverse to make past, but past is like for like.

22) **Adult**
    Fame

Quest can be coded for by search as adult and fame are more important. Child can be coded for by combining opposite and adult. Baby would mean something different to child.

23) **Make**
    Past

The is not necessary in codes in general. Ground is not necessary as sand is already a code. Shone is not in the message.

24) **Contain**
Desert

Opposite quick can code for long. Are is not necessary for codes in general. Storms can be coded for by many storm.

25) **Must**
Strong

And and Be are not necessary for codes in general. There is no reference to he in the message.

26) **Require**
Grow

Want is not a replacement for need, as they mean different things – require is better. To is not necessary for the message to make sense in code. Liquid is not necessary as water is already a code.

SITUATIONAL JUDGMENT TEST

Your ethical and moral outlook to see if you have the qualities to become a good medical profession

This section is the Situational Judgment Tests practice question, we recommend you refresh your memory on how to approach this section on pages 46 - 51

What is expected of you?

This subtest encompasses the non-cognitive part of the test. It measures your capacity to understand real world situations and gauges you behaviour while dealing with them. There will be 27 minutes to get through 71 items each of which will have a range of between 3-6 response options. It consists of a series of scenarios with possible actions and considerations. Being non-cognitive, it does not require any prior knowledge or understanding of the scenarios but simply analysing the best course of action for a given scenario.

The first set of questions will require you to rate the appropriateness of a number of options in relation to the given scenario.

When considering how to respond to the scenario, an option is:
- *a very appropriate thing to do* if it will applies to at least one aspect (not necessarily all aspects) of the situation
- *appropriate, but not ideal* if it could be done, but is not fundamentally a very good thing to do

- *inappropriate, **but not awful*** if it should not really be done, but would not be atrocious
- *a very inappropriate thing to do* if it should definitely not be done and would make the situation worse

The response in this case should not be considered as if it were the only thing that would be done. For instance, if a patient is allergic to paracetamol but is given it by accident, there are a number of steps to undertake, which include ascertaining that the patient is alright, evaluating the patient medically etc In this scenario, a response of ' ask the patient if they are ok' should still be judged as appropriate instead of seeing it as the ONLY action that will be taken.

The second set of questions will require you to rate the importance of a number of options in response to a given scenario.

. When considering how to respond to the scenario, an option is:
- *very important* if this is something that is crucial to take into account
- *important* if this is something that is imperative but not crucial to take into account
- *of minor importance* if this is something that could be taken into account, but its significance is questionable
- *not important at all* if this is something that should not be taken into account under any circumstances

Top tips! (based on the official UKCAT guide 2013)

1. It is important to relate your responses to what an individual *should* do, rather than what they may be likely to do.
2. Response options should be considered separately. You should make a judgement as to the appropriateness or importance of a response option independent from the other options presented within the scenario. This is difficult but with practice, you'll learn how to do this.
3. The options provided do not correspond to all possible options for a given scenario. Therefore, what would have ideally been the most appropriate/most important response according to you, may not be present in the given question
4. Don't worry too much about the time frame of the response.
a) Some options may be appropriate/important in the *short term* (i.e. immediately addressing a wrong doing) and some are appropriate/important in the *long term* (discussing the implications of the wrong doing after the event). Consider response options irrelevant of the time frame. A response option may still be an appropriate thing to do even if it is not something that can be done immediately.
1. Take a moment to think before you answer and ensure that you have read the question thoroughly.
a) We advise that you learn the implications of each of the options so that it will be easier for you to answer these questions, for instance, *appropriate, **but not ideal*** implies that it could be done, but is not fundamentally a very good thing to do etc

Question 1

A patient suffering from dementia is undergoing an examination, but suddenly becomes agitated and angry. How appropriate are each of the following responses.

1) Continue with the examination –

   A very appropriate thing to do

   Appropriate, but not ideal

   Inappropriate, but not awful

   A very inappropriate thing to do

2) Wait until the patient calms down before continuing –

   A very appropriate thing to do

   Appropriate, but not ideal

   Inappropriate, but not awful

   A very inappropriate thing to do

3) Ask his partner to calm him down before continuing –

   A very appropriate thing to do

   Appropriate, but not ideal

   Inappropriate, but not awful

   A very inappropriate thing to do

4) Suggest to his partner that they book another appointment at a later date –

   A very appropriate thing to do

   Appropriate, but not ideal

   Inappropriate, but not awful

   A very inappropriate thing to do

5) Try and elicit the cause of the agitation and calm the patient down –

   A very appropriate thing to do

   Appropriate, but not ideal

   Inappropriate, but not awful

   A very inappropriate thing to do

Question 2

Joe has recently been missing deadlines for handing in some work at his university. His tutor has threatened to kick him off the course if this happens once more without good reason. James knows that Joe has been having some family trouble recently, and this is the likely cause of him missing his deadlines; however Joe has not mentioned this to his tutor. How appropriate are each of the following responses.

1) James tells the university about Joe's family trouble -

   A very appropriate thing to do

   Appropriate, but not ideal

   Inappropriate, but not awful

   A very inappropriate thing to do

2) James speaks to Joe about why he doesn't want to divulge his family issues -

   A very appropriate thing to do

   Appropriate, but not ideal

   Inappropriate, but not awful

   A very inappropriate thing to do

3) James offers to help Joe with his work -

   A very appropriate thing to do

   Appropriate, but not ideal

Inappropriate, but not awful

A very inappropriate thing to do

4) James does nothing -

A very appropriate thing to do

Appropriate, but not ideal

Inappropriate, but not awful

A very inappropriate thing to do

5) James asks Joe if he can help in anyway -

A very appropriate thing to do

Appropriate, but not ideal

Inappropriate, but not awful

A very inappropriate thing to do

Question 3

Ben and Sylvia are both in the same problem solving group. They have been discussing a sensitive current case study. Ben has made some disparaging comments about people involved in the case study which Sylvie thinks are extremely offensive. How appropriate are each of the following responses.

1) Sylvie confronts Ben in front of the group

A very appropriate thing to do

Appropriate, but not ideal

Inappropriate, but not awful

A very inappropriate thing to do

2) Sylvie waits until the end of the session and then asks Ben not to make the comments

A very appropriate thing to do

Appropriate, but not ideal

Inappropriate, but not awful

A very inappropriate thing to do

3) Sylvie does nothing –

A very appropriate thing to do

Appropriate, but not ideal

Inappropriate, but not awful

A very inappropriate thing to do

4) Sylvie tells their supervisor what has happened –

A very appropriate thing to do

Appropriate, but not ideal

Inappropriate, but not awful

A very inappropriate thing to do

5) Sylvie confides in her friend who is also in the same group and asks her what to do

A very appropriate thing to do

Appropriate, but not ideal

Inappropriate, but not awful

A very inappropriate thing to do

Question 4

A recent complaint by a patient has led to a newspaper investigation into death rates at a hospital. Sarah has read some articles and tells the doctor she wishes to be treated at a different hospital as she believes she would be cared for better elsewhere. How appropriate are each of the following responses.

1) The doctor tells her that the newspaper reports are wrong

A very appropriate thing to do

Appropriate, but not ideal

Inappropriate, but not awful

A very inappropriate thing to do

2) The doctor assures her that the staff make every effort to provide a quality service

A very appropriate thing to do

Appropriate, but not ideal

Inappropriate, but not awful

A very inappropriate thing to do

3) Tell Sarah that he will look into the evidence

A very appropriate thing to do

Appropriate, but not ideal

Inappropriate, but not awful

A very inappropriate thing to do

4) Ask Sarah why she thinks this

A very appropriate thing to do

Appropriate, but not ideal

Inappropriate, but not awful

A very inappropriate thing to do

5) Allow Sarah to go to a different hospital

A very appropriate thing to do

Appropriate, but not ideal

Inappropriate, but not awful

A very inappropriate thing to do

Two medical students, John and Dave, take a history of a patient together, but come up with different diagnoses before the examination. Dave is sure he is correct, whilst John isn't so confident. How appropriate are each of the following responses.

1) Dave explains to John in front of the patient why he is correct

A very appropriate thing to do

Appropriate, but not ideal

Inappropriate, but not awful

A very inappropriate thing to do

2) Dave waits until the end of the consultation before explaining to John why he is correct

A very appropriate thing to do

Appropriate, but not ideal

Inappropriate, but not awful

A very inappropriate thing to do

3) John questions Dave in front of the patient

A very appropriate thing to do

Appropriate, but not ideal

Inappropriate, but not awful

A very inappropriate thing to do

4) They call a senior doctor before continuing

A very appropriate thing to do

Appropriate, but not ideal

Inappropriate, but not awful

A very inappropriate thing to do

5) They continue on with the examination

A very appropriate thing to do

Appropriate, but not ideal

Inappropriate, but not awful

A very inappropriate thing to do

Question 6

A patient has just undergone surgery and has been asked by the doctors to stay in hospital for the next week for observation. A medical student is sitting with the patient when he asks to leave as he needs to look after his elderly mother. There are no doctors available at the time. How appropriate are each of the following responses.

1)　The medical student tells the patient he cannot leave -

A very appropriate thing to do

Appropriate, but not ideal

Inappropriate, but not awful

A very inappropriate thing to do

2)　The medical student reminds the patient of what the doctor has said

A very appropriate thing to do

Appropriate, but not ideal

Inappropriate, but not awful

A very inappropriate thing to do

3) The medical student tells the patient to ask a nurse

A very appropriate thing to do

Appropriate, but not ideal

Inappropriate, but not awful

A very inappropriate thing to do

4) The medical student allows the patient to leave

A very appropriate thing to do

Appropriate, but not ideal

Inappropriate, but not awful

A very inappropriate thing to do

5) The medical student asks the patient to wait until a doctor is present

A very appropriate thing to do

Appropriate, but not ideal

Inappropriate, but not awful

A very inappropriate thing to do

Question 7

Jermaine, a medical student, is talking to a patient at a General Practice. He has been given her notes by the GP. The patient confides in Jermaine that she is worried that she is soon going to begin a course of new steroids; however Jermaine has been told by the GP that the patient's medication is not being changed. How appropriate are each of the following responses.

1) Jermaine asks the patient why she is worried

A very appropriate thing to do

Appropriate, but not ideal

Inappropriate, but not awful

A very inappropriate thing to do

2) Jermaine tells the GP the patient's concerns

A very appropriate thing to do

Appropriate, but not ideal

Inappropriate, but not awful

A very inappropriate thing to do

3) Jermaine suggests to the patient that she voice her concerns to the GP

A very appropriate thing to do

Appropriate, but not ideal

Inappropriate, but not awful

A very inappropriate thing to do

4) Jermaine tells the patient that she is not going to begin a new course

A very appropriate thing to do

Appropriate, but not ideal

Inappropriate, but not awful

A very inappropriate thing to do

5) Jermaine tells the patient she has nothing to worry about

A very appropriate thing to do

Appropriate, but not ideal

Inappropriate, but not awful

A very inappropriate thing to do

Question 8

Kirti is clinical partners with Andrew. Recently, Kirti has noticed Andrew making mistakes during patient examinations, not explaining procedures to patients and various other issues that he needs to improve upon. Some patients have picked up on his mistakes and seem uncomfortable. How appropriate are each of the following responses.

1) Kirti mentions to Andrew privately that he has been making mistakes

A very appropriate thing to do

Appropriate, but not ideal

Inappropriate, but not awful

A very inappropriate thing to do

2) Kirti mentions to their supervisor that Andrew has been making mistakes

A very appropriate thing to do

Appropriate, but not ideal

Inappropriate, but not awful

A very inappropriate thing to do

3) Kirti apologises to the patients

A very appropriate thing to do

Appropriate, but not ideal

Inappropriate, but not awful

A very inappropriate thing to do

4) Kirti points out Andrew's mistakes in front of the patient

A very appropriate thing to do

Appropriate, but not ideal

Inappropriate, but not awful

A very inappropriate thing to do

5) Kirti does nothing as Andrew's mistakes are not affecting the patient's health

A very appropriate thing to do

Appropriate, but not ideal

Inappropriate, but not awful

A very inappropriate thing to do

An FY2 doctor has been asked to temporarily oversee a medical student taking a patient examination. During the examination, the doctor notices something that the medical student has missed. After pointing this out, the student is still unable to locate the problem. How appropriate are each of the following responses.

1) The doctor shows the student where the problem lies

   A very appropriate thing to do

   Appropriate, but not ideal

   Inappropriate, but not awful

   A very inappropriate thing to do

2) The doctor takes over the examination

   A very appropriate thing to do

   Appropriate, but not ideal

   Inappropriate, but not awful

   A very inappropriate thing to do

3) The doctor waits until the end of the examination before further explaining the problem

   A very appropriate thing to do

   Appropriate, but not ideal

   Inappropriate, but not awful

   A very inappropriate thing to do

4) The doctor tells the students overseer what has happened

   A very appropriate thing to do

   Appropriate, but not ideal

   Inappropriate, but not awful

   A very inappropriate thing to do

5) The doctor does nothing else as the student is lacking in knowledge

   A very appropriate thing to do

   Appropriate, but not ideal

   Inappropriate, but not awful

   A very inappropriate thing to do

Question 10

An interprofessional student group is working on an assessed project together. They are overseen by a member of staff who will also assess them on their teamwork skills. Nikita notices that Clara has not made any contributions, and this is affecting the quality of their project. How appropriate are each of the following responses.

1) Nikita confronts Clara in front of the whole group

   A very appropriate thing to do

   Appropriate, but not ideal

   Inappropriate, but not awful

   A very inappropriate thing to do

2) Nikita suggests that they all take turns to talk

   A very appropriate thing to do

   Appropriate, but not ideal

   Inappropriate, but not awful

   A very inappropriate thing to do

3) Nikita tells the member of staff her feelings

A very appropriate thing to do

Appropriate, but not ideal

Inappropriate, but not awful

A very inappropriate thing to do

4) Nikita asks Clara privately why she isn't contributing

A very appropriate thing to do

Appropriate, but not ideal

Inappropriate, but not awful

A very inappropriate thing to do

5) Nikita does nothing -

A very appropriate thing to do

Appropriate, but not ideal

Inappropriate, but not awful

A very inappropriate thing to do

Question 11

Shaniqua and Chantelle are two dental students sitting in a class. Chantelle notices Shaniqua has answered a question wrong in her tutorial, and nudges her to point the mistake out. Shaniqua subsequently gets angry at Chantelle for reading her work and whispers rude comments to her. The teacher overhears this and directs a rude and offensive joke at Shaniqua in front of the whole class. Chantelle is stunned by the lecturers comments, and Shaniqua walks out. How appropriate are each of the following responses.

1) Chantelle checks whether Shaniqua is okay

A very appropriate thing to do

Appropriate, but not ideal

Inappropriate, but not awful

A very inappropriate thing to do

2) Chantelle confronts the teacher in front of the class

A very appropriate thing to do

Appropriate, but not ideal

Inappropriate, but not awful

A very inappropriate thing to do

3) Chantelle questions the teacher's comments after the class has ended

A very appropriate thing to do

Appropriate, but not ideal

Inappropriate, but not awful

A very inappropriate thing to do

4) Chantelle tells the university what the teacher did

A very appropriate thing to do

Appropriate, but not ideal

Inappropriate, but not awful

A very inappropriate thing to do

5) Chantelle reports Shaniqua for making rude comments

A very appropriate thing to do

Appropriate, but not ideal

Inappropriate, but not awful

A very inappropriate thing to do

Arjoon and Grace both recently took practice clinical exams. Although they felt they performed similarly, Grace received more negative comments than Arjoon, which she thought was unfair. How appropriate are each of the following responses.

1) Arjoon asks Grace why she feels the comments are unfair

   A very appropriate thing to do

   Appropriate, but not ideal

   Inappropriate, but not awful

   A very inappropriate thing to do

2) Arjoon tells the examiner that Grace is unhappy

   A very appropriate thing to do

   Appropriate, but not ideal

   Inappropriate, but not awful

   A very inappropriate thing to do

3) Arjoon offers to help Grace with her clinical skills

   A very appropriate thing to do

   Appropriate, but not ideal

   Inappropriate, but not awful

   A very inappropriate thing to do

4) Arjoon does nothing -

   A very appropriate thing to do

   Appropriate, but not ideal

   Inappropriate, but not awful

   A very inappropriate thing to do

5) Arjoon suggests Grace request further feedback

   A very appropriate thing to do

   Appropriate, but not ideal

   Inappropriate, but not awful

   A very inappropriate thing to do

A doctor has asked Anna, a medical student to take a history of a patient at a practice. The patient mentions a new medication that her friend in America, who is a doctor, suggested she try out. She asks Anna to give her information about the new medication. How appropriate are each of the following responses.

1) Anna tells the patient she does not know about this new medication

   A very appropriate thing to do

   Appropriate, but not ideal

   Inappropriate, but not awful

   A very inappropriate thing to do

2) Anna tells the patient she will research the medication and provide her with information

   A very appropriate thing to do

   Appropriate, but not ideal

   Inappropriate, but not awful

   A very inappropriate thing to do

3) Anna asks the patient why she wants to take the new medication

   A very appropriate thing to do

   Appropriate, but not ideal

   Inappropriate, but not awful

A very inappropriate thing to do

4) Anna suggests to the patient that she ask the GP about the new medication

A very appropriate thing to do

Appropriate, but not ideal

Inappropriate, but not awful

A very inappropriate thing to do

5) Anna tells the GP about the new medication

A very appropriate thing to do

Appropriate, but not ideal

Inappropriate, but not awful

A very inappropriate thing to do

Question 14

Jenny, a medical student, is in a patient consultation. She calls a senior doctor, to whom the patient starts complaining to about Jenny's manner. How appropriate are each of the following responses.

1) The doctor apologises to patient for Jenny's manner

A very appropriate thing to do

Appropriate, but not ideal

Inappropriate, but not awful

A very inappropriate thing to do

2) The doctor asks Jenny to leave

A very appropriate thing to do

Appropriate, but not ideal

Inappropriate, but not awful

A very inappropriate thing to do

3) The doctor asks the patient what Jenny has done wrong

A very appropriate thing to do

Appropriate, but not ideal

Inappropriate, but not awful

A very inappropriate thing to do

4) The doctor asks Jenny what she has done wrong

A very appropriate thing to do

Appropriate, but not ideal

Inappropriate, but not awful

A very inappropriate thing to do

5) The doctor observes the rest of the consultation

A very appropriate thing to do

Appropriate, but not ideal

Inappropriate, but not awful

A very inappropriate thing to do

Question 15

Maya and Tammy, two nursing students have to write an essay on a lecture that was given recently. Maya missed the lecture, and asks Tammy to send her the essay as she does not understand the topic. She says she will not copy the essay. Tammy however isn't sure whether she will copy it or not. How appropriate are each of the following responses.

1) Tammy sends Maya the essay

A very appropriate thing to do

Appropriate, but not ideal

Inappropriate, but not awful

A very inappropriate thing to do

2) Tammy offers to help Maya understand the topic

A very appropriate thing to do

Appropriate, but not ideal

Inappropriate, but not awful

A very inappropriate thing to do

3) Tammy refuses to help Maya -

A very appropriate thing to do

Appropriate, but not ideal

Inappropriate, but not awful

A very inappropriate thing to do

4) Tammy complains to their tutor about Maya

A very appropriate thing to do

Appropriate, but not ideal

Inappropriate, but not awful

A very inappropriate thing to do

5) Tammy offers to help Maya write the essay

A very appropriate thing to do

Appropriate, but not ideal

Inappropriate, but not awful

A very inappropriate thing to do

Question 16

A dental student, Rachel, is observing a dentist in the clinic when he swears audibly in front of the patient. It was not directed at anyone. How appropriate are

each of the following responses.

1) Rachel apologises to the patient immediately

A very appropriate thing to do

Appropriate, but not ideal

Inappropriate, but not awful

A very inappropriate thing to do

2) Once the patient leaves, Rachel tells the dentist that his language is inappropriate

A very appropriate thing to do

Appropriate, but not ideal

Inappropriate, but not awful

A very inappropriate thing to do

3) Rachel tells the dentist not to swear -

A very appropriate thing to do

Appropriate, but not ideal

Inappropriate, but not awful

A very inappropriate thing to do

4) Rachel does not comment as the patient does not complain

A very appropriate thing to do

Appropriate, but not ideal

Inappropriate, but not awful

A very inappropriate thing to do

5) Rachel reports the dentist to a senior member of staff

A very appropriate thing to do

Appropriate, but not ideal

Inappropriate, but not awful

A very inappropriate thing to do

Question 17

Two medical students, Michael and Steve are asked to take a patient's history together. When they see the patient, Michael immediately takes over and asks the patient questions, not allowing Steve to contribute. How appropriate are each of the following responses.

1) Steve does nothing as Michael is doing well

A very appropriate thing to do

Appropriate, but not ideal

Inappropriate, but not awful

A very inappropriate thing to do

2) At the end of the history, Steve complains to his tutor

A very appropriate thing to do

Appropriate, but not ideal

Inappropriate, but not awful

A very inappropriate thing to do

3) At the end of the history, Steve asks Michael to share the time evenly

A very appropriate thing to do

Appropriate, but not ideal

Inappropriate, but not awful

A very inappropriate thing to do

4) Steve interrupts Michael as he has an important question to ask

A very appropriate thing to do

Appropriate, but not ideal

Inappropriate, but not awful

A very inappropriate thing to do

5) Steve politely asks Michael to let him ask the patient a question

A very appropriate thing to do

Appropriate, but not ideal

Inappropriate, but not awful

A very inappropriate thing to do

Question 18

James has a meeting with his personal tutor in a week's time. However he has just found out that he has to take his grandmother to the hospital at the same time. Ben offers to switch with him. How appropriate are each of the following responses.

1) James switches times with Ben

A very appropriate thing to do

Appropriate, but not ideal

Inappropriate, but not awful

A very inappropriate thing to do

2) James email's the tutor asking if he can switch with Ben

A very appropriate thing to do

Appropriate, but not ideal

Inappropriate, but not awful

A very inappropriate thing to do

3) James asks his grandmother to reschedule the appointment as his meeting is very important

A very appropriate thing to do

Appropriate, but not ideal

Inappropriate, but not awful

A very inappropriate thing to do

4) James email's the tutor explaining his circumstance and asks to reschedule

A very appropriate thing to do

Appropriate, but not ideal

Inappropriate, but not awful

A very inappropriate thing to do

5) James asks Ben to let their tutor know he will not be able to make the meeting

A very appropriate thing to do

Appropriate, but not ideal

Inappropriate, but not awful

A very inappropriate thing to do

Question 19

A patient at a general practice has been waiting for an hour to see his doctor. He has become rather agitated and angry, and begins to complain loudly to the receptionist. The receptionist asks him to calm down and take a seat, at which point he shouts at her. The doctor walks in at this point. How important to take into account are the following considerations when deciding how to respond to the situation?

1) The safety of the receptionist

Very important

Important

Of minor importance

Not important at all

2) The safety of the other patients

Very important

Important

Of minor importance

Not important at all

3) The patient's feelings -

Very important

Important

Of minor importance

Not important at all

4) The patient's health

Very important

Important

Of minor importance

Not important at all

5) The amount of people waiting to be seen

Very important

Important

Of minor importance

Not important at all

Question 20

An FY1 doctor is working in A&E when a patient comes in with a complaint. After examining the patient, the doctor is unable to make a diagnosis. The A&E ward is full. How important to take into account are the following considerations when deciding how to respond to the situation?

1) The patient is still not feeling well

Very important

Important

Of minor importance

Not important at all

2) A&E is very busy

Very important

Important

Of minor importance

Not important at all

3) The view of a senior doctor

Very important

Important

Of minor importance

Not important at all

4) The view of a junior doctor

Very important

Important

Of minor importance

Not important at all

5) The view of a nurse

Very important

Important

Of minor importance

Not important at all

Question 21

Imran is attending a compulsory clinical skills session when he notices Diana signing in another student who is not present. Diana asks Imran to keep quiet about what she is doing. How important to take into account are the following considerations when deciding how to respond to the situation?

1) Diana has asked him to keep quiet

Very important

Important

Of minor importance

Not important at all

2) The other student will attend a different clinical skills session

Very important

Important

Of minor importance

Not important at all

3) If they are caught they will be in trouble

Very important

Important

Of minor importance

Not important at all

4) Imran himself did not sign in the other student

Very important

Important

Of minor importance

Not important at all

5) The other student could not attend due to a family emergency

Very important

Important

Of minor importance

Not important at all

Question 22

Jenson and Lewis are sitting in a tutorial. Lewis is eating crisps, and when the tutor notices, he tells Lewis off as it is against the rules, and asks him to leave. Jenson knows that the tutor normally does not mind people eating in her tutorials, and thinks it prejudiced that Lewis has to leave. How important to take into account are the following considerations when deciding how to respond to the situation?

1) Eating is against the rules

Very important

Important

Of minor importance

Not important at all

2) The tutor does not normally mind

Very important

Important

Of minor importance

Not important at all

3) The tutor has picked on Lewis before

Very important

Important

Of minor importance

Not important at all

4) Lewis was not disrupting the class

Very important

Important

Of minor importance

Not important at all

5) The tutor answered his mobile phone in the tutorial, which is also against the rules

Very important

Important

Of minor importance

Not important at all

Question 23

A patient is dying from a rare cancer. There is a drug available that may have some effect in combatting the cancer, however it is extremely expensive. How important to take into account are the following considerations when deciding how to respond to the situation?

1) The cost of the drug

Very important

Important

Of minor importance

Not important at all

2) How effective the drug is

Very important

Important

Of minor importance

Not important at all

3) The patient's wishes

Very important

Important

Of minor importance

Not important at all

4) The daughter of the patient's wishes

Very important

Important

Of minor importance

Not important at all

5) The time it would take to procure and adminis-
ter the drug

Very important

Important

Of minor importance

Not important at all

Question 24

A doctor is asked by a terminal patient's family to give

life sustaining treatment. The doctor knows that the
treatment will only prolong the patient's life for a few
days, after which he will die regardless. How important to take into account are the following considerations when deciding how to respond to the situation?

1) The patient's wishes

Very important

Important

Of minor importance

Not important at all

2) The wishes of the patient's family

Very important

Important

Of minor importance

Not important at all

3) The views of the other senior doctors

Very important

Important

Of minor importance

Not important at all

4) The cost of the treatment

Very important

Important

Of minor importance

Not important at all

5) The view of the hospital ethics board

Very important

Important

Of minor importance

Not important at all

A senior doctor asks a junior doctor to undertreat a patient's pain for fear of addiction. How important to take into account are the following considerations when deciding how to respond to the situation?

1) The amount of pain the patient is in

Very important

Important

Of minor importance

Not important at all

2) The views of the senior doctor

Very important

Important

Of minor importance

Not important at all

3) The views of the nurses

Very important

Important

Of minor importance

Not important at all

4) The type of pain medication being given

Very important

Important

Of minor importance

Not important at all

5) The junior doctor's personal views

Very important

Important

Of minor importance

Not important at all

Question 26

A doctor in charge of an adult patient has just found out that the patient is terminally ill. He is deciding whether to hide the information to improve the patient's spirit. How important to take into account are the following considerations when deciding how to respond to the situation?

1) The patient's spirit is likely to influence his health

Very important

Important

Of minor importance

Not important at all

2) The wishes of the patient's family

Very important

Important

Of minor importance

Not important at all

3) The right of the patient to know about his health

Very important

Important

Of minor importance

Not important at all

4) How long the patient has to live

Very important

Important

Of minor importance

Not important at all

5) Whether there are any treatments available to prolong the patient's life

Very important

Important

Of minor importance

Not important at all

Question 27

Dr. Selvakumar made a mistake during an examination, but it did not cause any physical harm to the patient. He is deciding whether to tell the patient his mistake. How important to take into account are the following considerations when deciding how to respond to the situation?

1) The patient was not harmed by the mistake

Very important

Important

Of minor importance

Not important at all

2) The doctor may be liable to litigation

Very important

Important

Of minor importance

Not important at all

3) The patient has a right to know what happened

Very important

Important

Of minor importance

Not important at all

4) The type of mistake made

Very important

Important

Of minor importance

Not important at all

5) It is the first time the he has made such a mistake

Very important

Important

Of minor importance

Not important at all

Question 28

A medical student overhears two doctors talking in the canteen about a case on the ward they were all working in. There does not seem to be any personal information disclosed during the conversation. How important to take into account are the following considerations when deciding how to respond to the situation?

1) The doctors have not done this before

Very important

Important

Of minor importance

Not important at all

2) The doctors did not mention any personal information

Very important

Important

Of minor importance

Not important at all

3) Both doctors were involved in the case

Very important

Important

Of minor importance

Not important at all

4) The doctors were in a public area where they could be overheard

Very important

Important

Of minor importance

Not important at all

5) The patient would not find out

Very important

Important

Of minor importance

Not important at all

A doctor has given John test results that indicate he has a sexually transmitted infection that is easily treated. John says he is sexually active with two different partners, and wears protection. He does not wish to tell either partner. Both of his partners are patients of the doctor. He is not sure whether he should tell them about John's results. How important to take into account are the following considerations when deciding how to respond to the situation?

1) John wears protection during intercourse

Very important

Important

Of minor importance

Not important at all

2) Both of John's partners are patients of the doctor

Very important

Important

Of minor importance

Not important at all

3) The STI is not a particularly dangerous one, and can be treated easily

Very important

Important

Of minor importance

Not important at all

4) John's right to confidentiality

Very important

Important

Of minor importance

Not important at all

5) John has not told either partner that he is sexually active with someone else

Very important

Important

Of minor importance

Not important at all

Dr. Patel is asked to perform an abortion, although it is against her beliefs. How important to take into account are the following considerations when deciding how to respond to the situation?

1) The wishes of the patient

Very important

Important

Of minor importance

Not important at all

2) Dr. Patel's own beliefs

Very important

Important

Of minor importance

Not important at all

3) The age of the fetus

Very important

Important

Of minor importance

Not important at all

4) The reason for the abortion

Very important

Important

Of minor importance

Not important at all

5) The views of other senior doctors

Very important

Important

Of minor importance

Not important at all

Question 31

Dr. Fillet has recently come back to work following the death of his wife. He has been making mistakes and receiving complaints from patients. The receptionist is worried after noticing alcohol on his breath which she thinks is from the previous night. She speaks to Dr. Jess about her concerns. How appropriate are each of the following responses.

1) Dr. Jess reassures the receptionist that Dr. Fillet is okay

A very appropriate thing to do

Appropriate, but not ideal

Inappropriate, but not awful

A very inappropriate thing to do

2) Dr. Jess speaks to Dr. Fillet and advises him to take some more time off

A very appropriate thing to do

Appropriate, but not ideal

Inappropriate, but not awful

A very inappropriate thing to do

3) Dr. Jess speaks to the GMC for advice without revealing Dr. Fillet's identity

A very appropriate thing to do

Appropriate, but not ideal

Inappropriate, but not awful

A very inappropriate thing to do

4) Dr. Jess asks the receptionist to voice her concerns directly to Dr. Fillet

A very appropriate thing to do

Appropriate, but not ideal

Inappropriate, but not awful

A very inappropriate thing to do

5) Dr. Jess reports Dr. Fillet to the GMC

A very appropriate thing to do

Appropriate, but not ideal

Inappropriate, but not awful

A very inappropriate thing to do

Question 32

A 14 year old girl comes to the GP to ask for contraception. She says she would like to start a sexual relationship with a 15 year old boy. How appropriate are each of the following responses.

1) The GP gives the girl an appropriate form of contraception

A very appropriate thing to do

Appropriate, but not ideal

Inappropriate, but not awful

A very inappropriate thing to do

2) The GP reports the boy and girl to the authorities

A very appropriate thing to do

Appropriate, but not ideal

Inappropriate, but not awful

A very inappropriate thing to do

3) The GP informs the girl's parent

A very appropriate thing to do

Appropriate, but not ideal

Inappropriate, but not awful

A very inappropriate thing to do

4) After finding the girl competent to make decisions, the GP explains to the girl the types of contraception available

A very appropriate thing to do

Appropriate, but not ideal

Inappropriate, but not awful

A very inappropriate thing to do

5) The GP asks the girl to bring her boyfriend in to see him

A very appropriate thing to do

Appropriate, but not ideal

Inappropriate, but not awful

A very inappropriate thing to do

A patient who speaks very little English is about to be told that he is suffering from cancer by his doctor. He will need immediate treatment. How appropriate are each of the following responses.

1) The doctor tells the patient that he is suffering from cancer

A very appropriate thing to do

Appropriate, but not ideal

Inappropriate, but not awful

A very inappropriate thing to do

2) The doctor asks the patient to bring a relative or friend in who can speak both languages

A very appropriate thing to do

Appropriate, but not ideal

Inappropriate, but not awful

A very inappropriate thing to do

3) The doctor reschedules the appointment to the earliest available opportunity where a professional translator can attend

A very appropriate thing to do

Appropriate, but not ideal

Inappropriate, but not awful

A very inappropriate thing to do

4) The doctor calls in a receptionist who is also a trained professional translator

A very appropriate thing to do

Appropriate, but not ideal

Inappropriate, but not awful

A very inappropriate thing to do

5) The doctor asks a fellow doctor who happens to speak the same language to translate

A very appropriate thing to do

Appropriate, but not ideal

Inappropriate, but not awful

A very inappropriate thing to do

Question 34

A 9 year old child has suffered a car accident, and is only able to breathe with a ventilator. He is fully paralysed, apart from being able to make eye movements, and there are no further treatment options available. The doctor in charge of his care has to decide what to do. How appropriate are each of the following responses.

1) The doctor removes the ventilator from the child and allow him to die with minimal suffering

A very appropriate thing to do

Appropriate, but not ideal

Inappropriate, but not awful

A very inappropriate thing to do

2) The doctor keeps him on the ventilator indefinitely

A very appropriate thing to do

Appropriate, but not ideal

Inappropriate, but not awful

A very inappropriate thing to do

3) The doctor asks the child's parents what they would like to do

A very appropriate thing to do

Appropriate, but not ideal

Inappropriate, but not awful

A very inappropriate thing to do

4) The doctor asks his colleagues for advice

A very appropriate thing to do

Appropriate, but not ideal

Inappropriate, but not awful

A very inappropriate thing to do

5) The doctor gets the child transported to another hospital where he will be more comfortable

A very appropriate thing to do

Appropriate, but not ideal

Inappropriate, but not awful

A very inappropriate thing to do

Question 35

A patient arrives in A&E. He immediately becomes angry and aggressive, and demands to be seen. A nurse asks him to calm down, at which point he begins to swear loudly. How appropriate are each of the following responses.

1) The nurse refuses to treat him -

A very appropriate thing to do

Appropriate, but not ideal

Inappropriate, but not awful

A very inappropriate thing to do

2) The nurse calls security

A very appropriate thing to do

Appropriate, but not ideal

Inappropriate, but not awful

A very inappropriate thing to do

3) The nurse calls the police

A very appropriate thing to do

Appropriate, but not ideal

Inappropriate, but not awful

A very inappropriate thing to do

4) The nurse treats him immediately

A very appropriate thing to do

Appropriate, but not ideal

Inappropriate, but not awful

A very inappropriate thing to do

5) The nurse restrains the patient

A very appropriate thing to do

Appropriate, but not ideal

Inappropriate, but not awful

A very inappropriate thing to do

Question 36

A doctor wishes to talk to a competent 15 year old about a particularly sensitive issue. He has come to the practice with his mother. The doctor feels that the child may be discouraged the child from being open. How appropriate are each of the following responses.

1) The doctor asks the child's mother to wait outside

A very appropriate thing to do

Appropriate, but not ideal

Inappropriate, but not awful

A very inappropriate thing to do

2) The doctor explains his belief to the child's mother and asks her to wait outside

A very appropriate thing to do

Appropriate, but not ideal

Inappropriate, but not awful

A very inappropriate thing to do

3) The doctor invites them both into the room

A very appropriate thing to do

Appropriate, but not ideal

Inappropriate, but not awful

A very inappropriate thing to do

4) The doctor asks the child if he would like his mother to come into the room with him

A very appropriate thing to do

Appropriate, but not ideal

Inappropriate, but not awful

A very inappropriate thing to do

5) The doctor reschedules the appointment for when the mother will not be there

A very appropriate thing to do

Appropriate, but not ideal

Inappropriate, but not awful

A very inappropriate thing to do

A patient is coming to the end of their life, but lacks the capacity to make decisions on any further treatment. Time is of the essence. How appropriate are each of the following responses.

1) The doctor tries to find out if he has any relatives

A very appropriate thing to do

Appropriate, but not ideal

Inappropriate, but not awful

A very inappropriate thing to do

2) The doctor makes all the necessary decisions, acting in the patient's best interests

A very appropriate thing to do

Appropriate, but not ideal

Inappropriate, but not awful

A very inappropriate thing to do

3) The doctor looks to see if the patient has a living will, or has made any decisions previously when able to do so

A very appropriate thing to do

Appropriate, but not ideal

Inappropriate, but not awful

A very inappropriate thing to do

4) The doctor makes decisions after consulting the patient's son

A very appropriate thing to do

Appropriate, but not ideal

Inappropriate, but not awful

A very inappropriate thing to do

5) The doctor asks his colleagues for guidance on the issue

A very appropriate thing to do

Appropriate, but not ideal

Inappropriate, but not awful

A very inappropriate thing to do

Question 38

A patient wishes to access a certain treatment, however the doctor does not believe it is the right treatment. After further discussion, and full explanation of all the options, the patient's view does not change. How appropriate are each of the following responses.

1) The doctor refuses to give treatment to the patient

A very appropriate thing to do

Appropriate, but not ideal

Inappropriate, but not awful

A very inappropriate thing to do

2) The doctor refuses to give the treatment, but gives guidance on obtaining a second opinion as well as getting legal help

A very appropriate thing to do

Appropriate, but not ideal

Inappropriate, but not awful

A very inappropriate thing to do

3) The doctor gives in to the patient's wishes

A very appropriate thing to do

Appropriate, but not ideal

Inappropriate, but not awful

A very inappropriate thing to do

4) The doctor asks his colleagues to speak to the patient

A very appropriate thing to do

Appropriate, but not ideal

Inappropriate, but not awful

A very inappropriate thing to do

5) The doctor tells the patient's family what has happened

A very appropriate thing to do

Appropriate, but not ideal

Inappropriate, but not awful

A very inappropriate thing to do

Question 39

A clinician in an important research trial for an anticancer drug has discovered the possibility of a seriously harmful side effect unknown up until this point. How appropriate are each of the following responses.

1) The clinician halts the trial immediately as there is life threatening risk to the trialists

A very appropriate thing to do

Appropriate, but not ideal

Inappropriate, but not awful

A very inappropriate thing to do

2) The clinician waits to see if the side effect occurs in any other trialists

A very appropriate thing to do

Appropriate, but not ideal

Inappropriate, but not awful

A very inappropriate thing to do

3) The clinician lets the trialists know of the possible side effect

A very appropriate thing to do

Appropriate, but not ideal

Inappropriate, but not awful

A very inappropriate thing to do

4) The clinician informs his colleagues of his discovery

A very appropriate thing to do

Appropriate, but not ideal

Inappropriate, but not awful

A very inappropriate thing to do

5) The clinician does not reveal any information as this would harm the integrity of the trial

A very appropriate thing to do

Appropriate, but not ideal

Inappropriate, but not awful

A very inappropriate thing to do

Question 40

A doctor's son has come in to A&E after an accident. How appropriate are each of the following responses.

1) He treats his son as he would any other patient

A very appropriate thing to do

Appropriate, but not ideal

Inappropriate, but not awful

A very inappropriate thing to do

2) He passes his son on to a colleague

A very appropriate thing to do

Appropriate, but not ideal

Inappropriate, but not awful

A very inappropriate thing to do

3) He asks his son to wait as his injury does not seem serious

A very appropriate thing to do

Appropriate, but not ideal

Inappropriate, but not awful

A very inappropriate thing to do

4) He lets his son move to the front of the waiting list

A very appropriate thing to do

Appropriate, but not ideal

Inappropriate, but not awful

A very inappropriate thing to do

5) He does not acknowledge his son as he is very busy

A very appropriate thing to do

Appropriate, but not ideal

Inappropriate, but not awful

A very inappropriate thing to do

A doctor is examining a patient with a head injury when the patient racially abuses her. The patient then complains that she is hurting him, and refuses to be treated by her. How appropriate are each of the following responses.

1) The doctor tells the patient that he has no alternative

A very appropriate thing to do

Appropriate, but not ideal

Inappropriate, but not awful

A very inappropriate thing to do

2) The doctor asks another colleague to take over and explains why

A very appropriate thing to do

Appropriate, but not ideal

Inappropriate, but not awful

A very inappropriate thing to do

3) The doctor asks the patient why he does not wish to be treated by her

A very appropriate thing to do

Appropriate, but not ideal

Inappropriate, but not awful

A very inappropriate thing to do

4) The doctor apologises for hurting the patient and explains it was not intentional

A very appropriate thing to do

Appropriate, but not ideal

Inappropriate, but not awful

A very inappropriate thing to do

5) The doctor reports the patient to the police

A very appropriate thing to do

Appropriate, but not ideal

Inappropriate, but not awful

A very inappropriate thing to do

Question 42

A patient comes in to the general practice and gives his doctor a gold watch worth around £500. How appropriate are each of the following responses.

1) The doctor accepts the gift and wears it in front of the patient

A very appropriate thing to do

Appropriate, but not ideal

Inappropriate, but not awful

A very inappropriate thing to do

2) The doctor accepts the gift but resolves not to wear it

A very appropriate thing to do

Appropriate, but not ideal

Inappropriate, but not awful

A very inappropriate thing to do

3) The doctor thanks the patient but politely refuses the gift

A very appropriate thing to do

Appropriate, but not ideal

Inappropriate, but not awful

A very inappropriate thing to do

4) The doctor explains that he is not allowed to accept such a gift from a patient of his

A very appropriate thing to do

Appropriate, but not ideal

Inappropriate, but not awful

A very inappropriate thing to do

5) The doctor accepts the gift but reports it to the GMC

A very appropriate thing to do

Appropriate, but not ideal

Inappropriate, but not awful

A very inappropriate thing to do

Question 43

A father comes in to the practice asking to see his 9 year old son's medical records. He is divorced from the child's mother (and does not have custody), and says that she refuses to tell him about the child's health. How appropriate are each of the following responses.

1) The father is refused access to the child's medical records

A very appropriate thing to do

Appropriate, but not ideal

Inappropriate, but not awful

A very inappropriate thing to do

2) The doctor asks the father and mother to come in to see him together before deciding what to do

A very appropriate thing to do

Appropriate, but not ideal

Inappropriate, but not awful

A very inappropriate thing to do

3) The doctor allows the father to see all of the child's medical records

A very appropriate thing to do

Appropriate, but not ideal

Inappropriate, but not awful

A very inappropriate thing to do

4) The doctor allows the father to see part of the child's records, but keeps any mention of the mother confidential

A very appropriate thing to do

Appropriate, but not ideal

Inappropriate, but not awful

A very inappropriate thing to do

5) The doctor calls the mother of the child to ask her if it is okay for the father to see the medical records

A very appropriate thing to do

Appropriate, but not ideal

Inappropriate, but not awful

A very inappropriate thing to do

Question 44

A nurse sees a patient in a bar 6 months after she helped treat him in hospital. The patient recognises her, and strikes up a conversation. They exchange numbers, and the patient later asks her out on a date. How appropriate are each of the following responses.

1) The nurse accepts the offer of the date as it has been 6 months since the one off treatment

A very appropriate thing to do

Appropriate, but not ideal

Inappropriate, but not awful

A very inappropriate thing to do

2) The nurse accepts the offer of the date but tells the patient that they would not be able to have a relationship

A very appropriate thing to do

Appropriate, but not ideal

Inappropriate, but not awful

A very inappropriate thing to do

3) The nurse politely refuses the offer of the date

A very appropriate thing to do

Appropriate, but not ideal

Inappropriate, but not awful

A very inappropriate thing to do

4) The nurse asks a colleague for advice

A very appropriate thing to do

Appropriate, but not ideal

Inappropriate, but not awful

A very inappropriate thing to do

5) The nurse consults the GMC for advice before responding

A very appropriate thing to do

Appropriate, but not ideal

Inappropriate, but not awful

A very inappropriate thing to do

A patient whose normal medication has been withdrawn from the market comes in to the GP to discuss a replacement. He has researched a new drug that is licensed in the US that he believes will suit him best. The doctor suggests a different drug based on the clinical guidelines; however the patient says that he tried this drug before and it wasn't as effective as the current one. How appropriate are each of the following responses.

1) The doctor insists that the patient tries the drug based on the clinical guidelines

A very appropriate thing to do

Appropriate, but not ideal

Inappropriate, but not awful

A very inappropriate thing to do

2) The doctor suggests that the patient try the drug based on the guidelines for a short period, while she researches the US licensed drug to see if it is suitable

A very appropriate thing to do

Appropriate, but not ideal

Inappropriate, but not awful

A very inappropriate thing to do

3) The doctor allows the patient to try the US licensed drug

A very appropriate thing to do

Appropriate, but not ideal

Inappropriate, but not awful

A very inappropriate thing to do

4) The doctor tells the patient that she does not know anything about the US licensed drug, so he cannot use it

A very appropriate thing to do

Appropriate, but not ideal

Inappropriate, but not awful

A very inappropriate thing to do

5) The doctor asks the patient why he wishes to try the US licensed drug

A very appropriate thing to do

Appropriate, but not ideal

Inappropriate, but not awful

A very inappropriate thing to do

Question 46

A 7 year old girl has been diagnosed with cancer, and is undergoing treatment. She has not yet been told of the nature of her illness (and has not asked). The parents ask the doctors not tell their daughter as they think it will cause her great distress.

1) The doctor tells the daughter as she has a right to know

A very appropriate thing to do

Appropriate, but not ideal

Inappropriate, but not awful

A very inappropriate thing to do

2) The doctor goes along with the parent's wishes

A very appropriate thing to do

Appropriate, but not ideal

Inappropriate, but not awful

A very inappropriate thing to do

3) The doctor first establishes if the daughter has the capacity to handle the information

A very appropriate thing to do

Appropriate, but not ideal

Inappropriate, but not awful

A very inappropriate thing to do

4) The doctor strikes up a conversation with the daughter to see if she has any interest in knowing about her illness

A very appropriate thing to do

Appropriate, but not ideal

Inappropriate, but not awful

A very inappropriate thing to do

5) The doctor believes that the girl has the capacity to understand the information, and that it will not distress her greatly, so tells her

A very appropriate thing to do

Appropriate, but not ideal

Inappropriate, but not awful

A very inappropriate thing to do

Question 47

A patient who suffered from an illness a few months ago phones in to ask her GP if she can prescribe her the same medication she used before. She says she has been fine since, but wants to have some by her in case the illness comes back while she goes on a long holiday. The medication in question is very addictive.

How appropriate are each of the following responses.

1) The GP asks the patient come into the practice for a consultation first

A very appropriate thing to do

Appropriate, but not ideal

Inappropriate, but not awful

A very inappropriate thing to do

2) The GP prescribes a small amount of the medication over the phone

A very appropriate thing to do

Appropriate, but not ideal

Inappropriate, but not awful

A very inappropriate thing to do

3) The GP prescribes a different, less addictive, medication over the phone

A very appropriate thing to do

Appropriate, but not ideal

Inappropriate, but not awful

A very inappropriate thing to do

4) The GP refuses to prescribe the medication

A very appropriate thing to do

Appropriate, but not ideal

Inappropriate, but not awful

A very inappropriate thing to do

5) The GP suggests she buy an 'over the counter' version at a pharmacy

A very appropriate thing to do

Appropriate, but not ideal

Inappropriate, but not awful

A very inappropriate thing to do

Question 48

A patient wishes to have further plastic surgery after having some a year before, but does not want the private surgeon to inform her GP. The surgeon wishes to contact the GP to establish if there are any other risks that may be pertinent. The patient refuses, and says that she knows the risks and that as she is paying, the surgeon should go ahead. How appropriate are each of the following responses.

1) The surgeon refuses to operate unless he is able to contact the GP

A very appropriate thing to do

Appropriate, but not ideal

Inappropriate, but not awful

A very inappropriate thing to do

2) The surgeon acquiesces to the patients request

A very appropriate thing to do

Appropriate, but not ideal

Inappropriate, but not awful

A very inappropriate thing to do

3) The surgeon asks the patient why she does not wish to contact her GP

A very appropriate thing to do

Appropriate, but not ideal

Inappropriate, but not awful

A very inappropriate thing to do

4) The surgeon goes ahead with the surgery, but contacts the GP first without the patient's knowledge

A very appropriate thing to do

Appropriate, but not ideal

Inappropriate, but not awful

A very inappropriate thing to do

5) The surgeon goes ahead with the surgery after re-explaining the risks

A very appropriate thing to do

Appropriate, but not ideal

Inappropriate, but not awful

A very inappropriate thing to do

Question 49

A mother comes in to the practice with her 8 year old child. She says her child is being bullied at school due to a large mole on his cheek, and wants to get it removed. She is divorced, and the child's father has not yet been informed. How appropriate are each of the following responses.

1) The doctor refers her and the child to a specialist

A very appropriate thing to do

Appropriate, but not ideal

Inappropriate, but not awful

A very inappropriate thing to do

2) The doctor asks the child his view

A very appropriate thing to do

Appropriate, but not ideal

Inappropriate, but not awful

A very inappropriate thing to do

3) The doctor asks the mother to first contact the father

A very appropriate thing to do

Appropriate, but not ideal

Inappropriate, but not awful

A very inappropriate thing to do

4) The doctor refuses to refer the mother and child as there is no physical benefit to the procedure

A very appropriate thing to do

Appropriate, but not ideal

Inappropriate, but not awful

A very inappropriate thing to do

5) The doctor asks the mother to contact the school to elicit the extent and reason of the bullying if known

A very appropriate thing to do

Appropriate, but not ideal

Inappropriate, but not awful

A very inappropriate thing to do

Question 50

A patient comes in with a mole which has recently begun to itch. The GP refers him to a dermatologist, who suggests they remove the mole so they can test it further. The dermatologist tells the patient that there may be some bleeding and he will need stitches. Upon hearing this, the patient tells the dermatologist that he doesn't want to know what it involves, and to just go ahead with treatment. How appropriate are each of the following responses.

1) The dermatologist has consent, so books the patient in for the procedure

A very appropriate thing to do

Appropriate, but not ideal

Inappropriate, but not awful

A very inappropriate thing to do

2) The dermatologist tells the patient that he must fully explain the risks before he can book the procedure

A very appropriate thing to do

Appropriate, but not ideal

Inappropriate, but not awful

A very inappropriate thing to do

3) The dermatologist continues with explaining the procedure

A very appropriate thing to do

Appropriate, but not ideal

Inappropriate, but not awful

A very inappropriate thing to do

4) The dermatologist does not book the patient in as he has not consented

A very appropriate thing to do

Appropriate, but not ideal

Inappropriate, but not awful

A very inappropriate thing to do

5) The dermatologist books the patient in, but asks the GP to explain the risks before the day of the procedure

A very appropriate thing to do

Appropriate, but not ideal

Inappropriate, but not awful

A very inappropriate thing to do

Question 51

A patient with a severe learning disability comes in with her mother to the GP. She has been agitated recently, and her mother is worried that something may be seriously wrong. How appropriate are each of the following responses.

1) The GP asks the mother what she thinks is wrong

A very appropriate thing to do

Appropriate, but not ideal

Inappropriate, but not awful

A very inappropriate thing to do

2) The GP asks the patient what she thinks is wrong

A very appropriate thing to do

Appropriate, but not ideal

Inappropriate, but not awful

A very inappropriate thing to do

3) The GP assesses the patients capacity to communicate before continuing with the consultation

A very appropriate thing to do

Appropriate, but not ideal

Inappropriate, but not awful

A very inappropriate thing to do

4) The GP asks a specially trained mental health nurse to be present during the consultation

A very appropriate thing to do

Appropriate, but not ideal

Inappropriate, but not awful

A very inappropriate thing to do

5) The GP asks the mother to wait outside while he continues with the consultation

A very appropriate thing to do

Appropriate, but not ideal

Inappropriate, but not awful

A very inappropriate thing to do

A 15 year old boy comes in to the GP wishing to see the doctor. It is against practice rules for children under 16 to be seen without their parent or guardian. However the boy refuses to leave and is clearly distressed. How appropriate are each of the following responses.

1) The GP makes an exception to the rule and sees the boy

A very appropriate thing to do

Appropriate, but not ideal

Inappropriate, but not awful

A very inappropriate thing to do

2) The GP asks a chaperone such as the practice receptionist to stay for the consultation, with the consent of the boy

A very appropriate thing to do

Appropriate, but not ideal

Inappropriate, but not awful

A very inappropriate thing to do

3) The GP refuses to see the boy as it is against practice rules

A very appropriate thing to do

Appropriate, but not ideal

Inappropriate, but not awful

A very inappropriate thing to do

4) The GP asks the patient why he does not wish to come in with his parent/guardian

A very appropriate thing to do

Appropriate, but not ideal

Inappropriate, but not awful

A very inappropriate thing to do

5) The GP waits until the waiting room is empty before seeing the boy

A very appropriate thing to do

Appropriate, but not ideal

Inappropriate, but not awful

A very inappropriate thing to do

SJT Answers

1. A patient suffering from dementia is undergoing an examination, but suddenly becomes agitated and angry. How appropriate are each of the following responses.

1) If the patient is not happy, the clinician should respect this and try and find out why and what can be done. **A very inappropriate thing to do**

2) The clinician should not continue until the patient calms down, but it may be better to actively do this rather passively wait. **Appropriate, but not ideal**

3) The patient is likely to be more comfortable with the person they came with. However it may not be possible to calm the patient, in which case the clinician should not automatically carry on. **Appropriate, but not ideal**

4) It may be difficult to reschedule, and the same issue could arise. First, the clinician should try to see if anything can be done to calm the patient down. **Inappropriate, but not awful**

5) It is important that the patient feel comfortable before any procedure. **A very appropriate thing to do**

2. Joe has recently been missing deadlines for handing in some work at his university. His tutor has threatened to kick him off the course if this happens once more without good reason. James knows that Joe has been having some family trouble recently, and this is the likely cause of him missing his deadlines; however Joe has not mentioned this to his tutor. How appropriate are each of the following responses.

1) James should not divulge Joe's personal information without his knowledge and permission. **A very inappropriate thing to do**

2) Offering Joe support is important. **A very inappropriate thing to do**

3) This would help Joe complete his work, however his work should be his own, and this would not solve the problem he faces. **Inappropriate, but not awful**

4) As it is not James' business, he does not need to get involved. However he should try and help Joe in any way he can. **Inappropriate, but not awful**

5) This is very appropriate as it does not cross boundaries and allows Joe to confide in him if he wishes. **A very appropriate thing to do**

3. Ben and Sylvia are both in the same problem solving group. They have been discussing a sensitive current case study. Ben has made some disparaging comments about people involved in the case study which Sylvie thinks are extremely offensive. How appropriate are each of the following responses.

1) Confronting Ben in front of the whole group would disrupt the team's ability to work together, and alienate the two of them. **A very inappropriate thing to do**

2) This allows her to make Ben aware of her feelings as well as allowing the chance of local resolution. **A very appropriate thing to do**

3) This is not the worst thing to do, however Ben's comments may be affecting other group members, and are clearly inappropriate so he should be made aware. **Inappropriate, but not awful**

4) Sylvie can do this in order to stop Joe from making the comments, however local resolution would be a better first option. **Inappropriate, but not awful**

5) Getting advice from a peer is a good strategy, however Ben may continue to make comments until he is made aware that Sylvie finds them offensive. **Appropriate, but not ideal**

4. A recent complaint by a patient has led to a newspaper investigation into death rates at a hospital. Sarah has read some articles and tells the doctor she wishes to be treated at a different hospital as she believes she would be cared for better elsewhere. How appropriate are each of the following responses.

1) The doctor does not know whether there is any truth to the reports, so this is essentially lying to the patient. **A very inappropriate thing to do**

2) This would help reassure the patient that she will be cared for well at the hospital. **A very appropriate thing to do**

3) It is important that he find out the truth so he can tell Sarah whether the reports are true or false. **A very appropriate thing to do**

4) This allows Sarah to feel she has been listened to, but does not solve the immediate problem of Sarah wishing to move to a different hospital. **Appropriate, but not ideal**

5) Ultimately, the doctor should allow the patient to move hospital, however he should first try and reassure her and find out whether there is any truth to the reports. **Inappropriate, but not awful**

5. Two medical students, John and Dave, take a history of a patient together, but come up with different diagnoses before the examination. Dave is sure he is correct, whilst John isn't so confident. How appropriate are each of the following responses.

1) This would allow John to understand what the problem is and the nature of the examination. However it may make the patient uncomfortable.**Appropriate, but not ideal**

2) This would allow John to understand in retrospect the examination process. However he would not be able to contribute and learn to the same extent as if he knew during the consultation. **Appropriate, but not ideal**

3) This is likely to make the patient uncomfortable as he will feel as if the medical students are not competent. **A very inappropriate thing to do**

4) This is a good course of action as the senior doctor would be best placed to provide an accurate diagnosis, as well as explain the reasoning. This would also make sure the patient is not put at any risk. **A very appropriate thing to do**

5) This would allow Dave to confirm his diagnosis, however the diagnosis may be inaccurate. Also, John would be unable to learn from the consultation. **Inappropriate, but not awful**

6. A patient has just undergone surgery and has been asked by the doctors to stay in hospital for the next week for observation. A medical student is sitting with the patient when he asks to leave as he needs to look after his elderly mother. There are no doctors available at the time. How appropriate are each of the following responses.

1) It is ultimately the patient's choice whether to leave – the medical student has no right to force the patient to stay.**A very inappropriate thing to do**

2) This is the best course of action as the medical student cannot give advice themself.**A very appropriate thing to do**

3) The nurse is not able to make a decision for the patient.**A very inappropriate thing to do**

4) The patient is within his rights to leave, however the medical student should first remind him of the doctor's recommendation.**Inappropriate, but not awful**

5) This is a good course of action as it allows the doctor to explain why the patient should stay. However the patient may need to leave urgently.**Appropriate, but not ideal**

7. Jermaine, a medical student, is talking to a patient at a General Practice. He has been given her notes by the GP. The patient confides in Jermaine that she is worried that she is soon going to begin a course of new steroids; however Jermaine has been told by the GP that the patient's medication is not being changed. How appropriate are each of the following responses.

1) This allows the patient to voice her concerns and feel listened to.**A very appropriate thing to do**

2) Jermaine shouldn't tell the GP without the patient's consent, however the patient's confidentiality would be protected.**Inappropriate, but not awful**

3) This allows the patient to get the best advice regarding what she is worried about.**A very appropriate thing to do**

4) Jermaine does not know whether there has been a change of plans, so should not tell the patient any assumptions he has made.**A very inappropriate thing to do**

5) Jermaine should not make any assumptions or statements if there is a change in the situation.**A very inappropriate thing to do**

8. Kirti is clinical partners with Andrew. Recently, Kirti has noticed Andrew making mistakes during patient examinations, not explaining procedures to patients and various other issues that he needs to improve upon. Some patients have picked up on his mistakes and seem uncomfortable. How appropriate are each of the following responses.

1) This makes sure Andrew is alerted to his mistakes, and allows him to make adjustments to improve.**A very appropriate thing to do**

2) This alerts the supervisor to Andrews mistakes, who can take steps to help Andrew. However Kirti should tell Andrew first.**Appropriate, but not ideal**

3) Kirti should not apologise on Andrew's behalf, as it undermines his authority.**A very inappropriate thing to do**

4) This would undermine Andrew's authority, however it would make sure that the patient is not harmed.**Appropriate, but not ideal**

5) Kirti should not stay silent as Andrew needs to learn the correct procedures. His mistakes may harm someone in the future.**A very inappropriate thing to do**

9. An FY2 doctor has been asked to temporarily oversee a medical student taking a patient examination. During the examination, the doctor notices something that the medical student has missed. After pointing this out, the student is still unable to locate the problem. How appropriate are each of the following responses.

1) This allows the student to learn.**A very appropriate thing to do**

2) This does not allow the student to learn, which is what the FY2 doctor has been asked to do.**Inappropriate, but not awful**

3) This would allow the medical student to learn, however the patient would not be properly examined.**Inappropriate, but not awful**

4) This is appropriate as the student's overseer will be able to take any steps necessary to help the student. However the FY2 doctor should also help the student at the time.**Appropriate, but not ideal**

5) This course of action means that the patient is not seen properly, and the student is not able to learn.**A very inappropriate thing to do**

10. An interprofessional student group is working on an assessed project together. They are overseen by a member of staff who will also assess them on their teamwork skills. Nikita notices that Clara has not made any contributions, and this is affecting the quality of their project. How appropriate are each of the following responses.

1) This would not help with their teamwork, and would alienate Clara. **A very inappropriate thing to do**

2) This would push Clara to contribute without confrontation.**A very appropriate thing to do**

3) This course of action would not solve the problem, however it could allow the member of staff to speak to Clara later.**Inappropriate, but not awful**

4) This allows Clara to explain herself without alienating her from the group.**A very appropriate thing to do**

5) This would not solve the problem of lack of teamwork.**Inappropriate, but not awful**

11. Shaniqua and Chantelle are two dental students sitting in a class. Chantelle notices Shaniqua has answered a question wrong in her tutorial, and nudges her to point the mistake out. Shaniqua subsequently gets angry at Chantelle for reading her work and whispers rude comments to her. The teacher overhears this and directs a rude and offensive joke at Shaniqua in front of the whole class. Chantelle is stunned by the lecturers comments, and Shaniqua walks out. How appropriate are each of the following responses.

1) It is important to check how Shaniqua is, and console her if she is distressed.**A very appropriate thing to do**

2) This would disrupt the rest of the class, and is better performed at the end of the session in private.**A very inappropriate thing to do**

3) This allows for local resolution.**A very appropriate thing to do**

4) The university should be alerted to wrongful behaviour of staff members.**A very appropriate thing to do**

5) If Chantelle is unhappy at Shaniqua she should tell a member of staff. However she should try and resolve the issue locally if possible first.**Inappropriate, but not awful**

12. Arjoon and Grace both recently took practice clinical exams. Although they felt they performed similarly, Grace received more negative comments than Arjoon, which she thought was unfair. How appropriate are each of the following responses.

1) This allows Grace to explain her feelings. **A very appropriate thing to do**

2) Arjoon should not break Grace's trust in him. Suggesting Grace talk to the examiner is a much better option. **A very inappropriate thing to do**

3) Arjoon should not assume that this is what Grace wants. **Inappropriate, but not awful**

4) This is not inappropriate, as he does not need to get involved. However he should offer to help her. **Appropriate, but not ideal**

5) This allows Grace to find out why she has not performed as well, without Arjoon breaking her trust. **A very appropriate thing to do**

13. A doctor has asked Anna, a medical student to take a history of a patient at a practice. The patient mentions a new medication that her friend in America, who is a doctor, suggested she try out. She asks Anna to give her information about the new medication. How appropriate are each of the following responses.

1) It is important to be truthful to the patient.**A very appropriate thing to do**

2) This will enable Anna to present the patient with the facts. However this could take a while.**Appropriate, but not ideal**

3) This allows the patient to feel listened to and explain herself.**A very appropriate thing to do**

4) The GP would be the best source of information on the topic.**A very appropriate thing to do**

5) This allows the GP to talk to the patient, however Anna should have asked the patients permission first.**Inappropriate, but not awful**

14. Jenny, a medical student, is in a patient consultation. She calls a senior doctor, to whom the patient starts complaining to about Jenny's manner. How appropriate are each of the following responses.

1) This assumes Jenny is in the wrong without establishing the facts.**Inappropriate, but not awful**

2) This assumes Jenny is in the wrong and does not allow her to explain herself.**A very inappropriate thing to do**

3) This allows the patient to explain their feelings, and helps the doctor establish what has happened.**A very appropriate thing to do**

4) The doctor should first listen to the patient who has complained.**Inappropriate, but not awful**

5) This will help reassure the patient, but assumes Jenny's guilt.**Appropriate, but not ideal**

15. Maya and Tammy, two nursing students have to write an essay on a lecture that was given recently. Maya missed the lecture, and asks Tammy to send her the essay as she does not understand the topic. She says she will not copy the essay. Tammy however isn't sure whether she will copy it or not. How appropriate are each of the following responses.

1) If Tammy feels Maya may plagiarise the essay, then she should not do this. If Maya does, then they will both be in trouble.**A very inappropriate thing to do**

2) This would allow Maya to write her essay without plagiarising.**A very appropriate thing to do**

3) If Tammy feels that Maya may plagiarise the essay, she is within her rights to say no. However she should try and offer to help Maya in some other way.**Appropriate, but not ideal**

4) Tammy should tell Maya what she thinks first. Maya has said she will not copy the essay.**A very inappropriate thing to do**

5) Maya's work should be her own. This is akin to plagiarism.**A very inappropriate thing to do**

16. A dental student, Rachel, is observing a dentist in the clinic when he swears audibly in front of the patient. It was not directed at anyone. How appropriate are each of the following responses.

1) Rachel should not apologise for the dentist as she has done nothing wrong.**A very inappropriate thing to do**

2) This alerts the dentist to what he has done.**A very appropriate thing to do**

3) Rachel should not demand the dentist to do anything, but should ask him.**Appropriate, but not ideal**

4) Regardless of the patients feelings, swearing is inappropriate and the dentist should be alerted to his behaviour.**A very inappropriate thing to do**

5) Rachel should first talk to the dentist before reporting it to a senior member of staff.**Appropriate, but not ideal**

17. Two medical students, Michael and Steve are asked to take a patient's history together. When they see the patient, Michael immediately takes over and asks the patient questions, not allowing Steve to contribute. How appropriate are each of the following responses.

1) This would allow the history to be performed well, but Michael would not gain anything from the session.**Appropriate, but not ideal**

2) Steve should first let Michael know what he thinks.**Appropriate, but not ideal**

3) This would solve the problem locally and allow them both to gain from the sessions.**A very appropriate thing to do**

4) This would disrupt the history take and they would both lose rapport with the patient.**A very inappropriate thing to do**

5) This allows Steve to ask his question without alienating Michael or the patient.**A very appropriate thing to do**

18. James has a meeting with his personal tutor in a week's time. However he has just found out that he has to take his grandmother to the hospital at the same time. Ben offers to switch with him. How appropriate are each of the following responses.

1) This would solve the problem, but he should also inform the tutor who may have prepared to see Ben.**Appropriate, but not ideal**

2) This would solve the problem and the tutor would be aware.**A very appropriate thing to do**

3) His grandmother's health is the most important concern. If he was to make his tutor aware of the situation there would probably be another way around the problem.**A very inappropriate thing to do**

4) This makes his tutor aware of the issue and solves the problem.**A very appropriate thing to do**

5) This makes the tutor aware of what has happened, however James should tell his tutor himself.**Inappropriate, but not awful**

19. A patient at a general practice has been waiting for an hour to see his doctor. He has become rather agitated and angry, and begins to complain loudly to the receptionist. The receptionist asks him to calm down and take a seat, at which point he shouts at her. The doctor walks in at this point. How important to take into account are the following considerations when deciding how to respond to the situation?

1) The safety of the receptionist should be of primary concern.**Very important**

2) The safety of the other patients should be of primary concern.**Very important**

3) It is important to acknowledge the patients

feelings.**Important**

4) It is important to acknowledge the patients health.**Important**

5) This should be taken into account as the doctor may wish to call the patient in immediately to calm him down.**Of minor importance**

20. An FY1 doctor is working in A&E when a patient comes in with a complaint. After examining the patient, the doctor is unable to make a diagnosis. The A&E ward is full. How important to take into account are the following considerations when deciding how to respond to the situation?

1) It is extremely important that the patient is seen to, as there could be a serious underlying condition.**Very important**

2) This is important as the longer the FY1 doctor spends with the once patient, the longer the other patients have to wait.**Important**

3) The senior doctor will have more experience and may be able to make a diagnosis.**Very important**

4) The advice of a peer may be useful, however a senior doctor is more likely to be able to help.**Of minor importance**

5) The nurse is unable to make a diagnosis in this situation.**Not important at all**

21. Imran is attending a compulsory clinical skills session when he notices Diana signing in another student who is not present. Diana asks Imran to keep quiet about what she is doing. How important to take into account are the following considerations when deciding how to respond to the situation?

1) It does not matter what Diana has asked him to do as what she is doing is against the rules.**Not important at all**

2) The fact that the other student will attend the session at a different time should be taken into account, but it does not excuse the fact that what is taking place is against the rules.**Of minor importance**

3) Imran should know the consequences of what they are doing.**Very important**

4) The fact that he has seen Diana do this means that he is almost as culpable.**Of minor importance**

5) It does not matter why the other student has attended. She could have explained herself to the tutor.**Not important at all**

22. Jenson and Lewis are sitting in a tutorial. Lewis is eating crisps, and when the tutor notices, he tells Lewis off as it is against the rules, and asks him to leave. Jenson knows that the tutor normally does not mind people eating in

her tutorials, and thinks it prejudiced that Lewis has to leave. How important to take into account are the following considerations when deciding how to respond to the situation?

1) Regardless of what Jenson feels, the fact that Lewis broke the rules is of utmost importance.**Very important**

2) The tutor has merely upheld the rules. The fact that he may be picking on a student does not change the fact that Lewis should not have been eating.**Of minor importance**

3) If there is a pattern developing then Lewis may feel the need to tell a senior member of staff what is going on.**Important**

4) Lewis has broken the rules, so it does not matter if he was disrupting the class.**Not important at all**

5) The tutor upheld the rules with regards to Lewis, which is the matter at hand. Jenson may wish to take up this other matter as well.**Of minor importance**

23. A patient is dying from a rare cancer. There is a drug available that may have some effect in combatting the cancer, however it is extremely expensive. How important to take into account are the following considerations when deciding how to respond to the situation?

1) The cost of the drug is important, as the NHS has limited funding. NICE produces guidelines on these issues.**Important**

2) This is very important as if the drug is not very effective it may be an inefficient use of resources.**Very important**

3) The patient has a right to have a say in the treatment he/she is given.**Very important**

4) The daughter is able to advise her mother/father, however the doctor should only listen to the patient.**Not important at all**

5) If the drug is not normally used, it may take a while to procure. However this should not play a major role in deciding whether to use it.**Of minor importance**

24. A doctor is asked by a terminal patient's family to give life sustaining treatment. The doctor knows that the treatment will only prolong the patient's life for a few days, after which he will die regardless. How important to take into account are the following considerations when deciding how to respond to the situation?

1) The patient has a right to decide what treatment is given.**Very important**

2) The patient's family are able to advise the patient, but ultimately it is between the patient and his doctor to decide any course of action.**Not important at all**

3) Other senior doctors would be able to provide ethical advice on the issue.**Important**

4) The cost needs to be taken into account as it may be a waste of resources. However this should not play a major role. **Of minor importance**.

5) The ethics board would be able to provide the best guidance on all ethical issues.**Very important**

25. A senior doctor asks a junior doctor to undertreat a patient's pain for fear of addiction. How important to take into account are the following considerations when deciding how to respond to the situation?

1) A doctor's duty is to do what is best for the patient. If the patient is in serious pain, the doctor should do what he can to alleviate the symptom.**Very important**

2) The senior doctor will have experience in the matter.**Important**

3) The nurses may be able to provide some insight into the patient.**Of minor importance**

4) Different medications have different levels of addiction associated with them.**Very important**

5) The junior doctor should not be forced into doing something he/she is not comfortable with.**Important**

26. A doctor in charge of an adult patient has just found out that the patient is terminally ill. He is deciding whether to hide the information to improve the patient's spirit. How important to take into account are the following considerations when deciding how to respond to the situation?

1) It may be better for the patient in the short term not to know if good spirits will improve his health.**Of minor importance**

2) The patient has the right to know before his/her family, so they should not have any input.**Not important at all**

3) The patient has a right to know what is going on.**Very important**

4) If the patient is going to die within days, then it may be better to tell him/her in order for them to sort out their affairs.**Important**

5) If there are such treatments, then the patient should have the ability to make an informed choice about what the next step is.**Very important**

27. Dr. Selvakumar made a mistake during an examination, but it did not cause any physical harm to the patient. He is deciding whether to tell the patient his mistake. How important to take into account are the following considerations when deciding how to respond to the situation?

1) If Dr. Selvakumar has not harmed the patient, then telling the patient may in fact result in more harm due to distress.**Of minor importance**

2) The doctor should do what is best for the patient, and not think about the personal consequences.**Not important at all**

3) The patient has a right to know about what has happened in his treatment.**Very important**

4) This is not very important as it may not matter to the patient.**Of minor importance**

5) Regardless of how many mistakes Dr. Selvakumar has made, he should not avoid telling the patient because it is a single time. This line of thought does not affect the patient.**Not important at all**

28. A medical student overhears two doctors talking in the canteen about a case on the ward they were all working in. There does not seem to be any personal information disclosed during the conversation. How important to take into account are the following considerations when deciding how to respond to the situation?

1) This may be a single incident, however if they accidentally break confidentiality, even once is too much.**Of minor importance**

2) If the doctors have not divulged personal information then they may not be doing anything wrong.**Important**

3) This means that they could be talking about the patient to further their care, however this is a minor detail.**Of minor importance**

4) This is very important as if they accidentally divulge personal information, it is open for anyone to hear.**Very important**

5) Regardless of whether the patient would find out, he/she has a right to confidentiality.**Not important at all**

29. A doctor has given John test results that indicate he has a sexually transmitted infection that is easily treated. John says he is sexually active with two different partners, and wears protection. He does not wish to tell either partner. Both of his partners are patients of the doctor. He is not sure whether he should tell them about John's results. How important to take into account are the following considerations when deciding how to respond to the situation?

1) When deciding whether to break confidentiality, it is important to consider what the harm would be if the doctor does not act. If John is wearing protection, then the possible harm is minimised, so should be taken into account.**Important**

2) This means that the doctor is able to contact the partners.

However this should not be the first thing considered.**Of minor importance**

3) When deciding whether to break confidentiality, it is important to consider what the harm would be if the doctor does not act. If the STI is not particularly dangerous, then the possible harm is minimised.**Important**

4) John has a right to confidentiality. Telling his partners would break the trust in the relationship.**Very important**

5) This is does not concern the doctor as it is John's private life.**Not important at all**

30. Dr. Patel is asked to perform an abortion, although it is against her beliefs. How important to take into account are the following considerations when deciding how to respond to the situation?

1) The patient is the one who is to be treated, so her wishes are of utmost importance.**Very important**

2) The patient's wishes are more important. However if she does not wish to perform the abortion she can pass the patient on to another colleague.**Of minor importance**

3) The age of fetus is important as it determines whether the abortion can be performed, and how.**Very important**

4) This is important as it will help inform the discussion between Dr. Patel and the patient over the issue of abortion.**Very important**

5) Other senior doctors can advise on the ethics and legality of the procedure. However an ethics board would/lawyer would be more suitable.**Important**

31. Dr. Fillet has recently come back to work following the death of his wife. He has been making mistakes and receiving complaints from patients. The receptionist is worried after noticing alcohol on his breath which she thinks is from the previous night. She speaks to Dr. Jess about her concerns. How appropriate are each of the following responses.

1) This is not appropriate as there is clearly an issue that needs to be addressed.**A very inappropriate thing to do**

2) This is appropriate, as this is likely the reason for Dr. Fillet's mistakes.**A very appropriate thing to do**

3) This is a good response as it protects Dr. Fillet's identity, and allows Dr. Jess to get help in deciding what to do from a reliable source.**A very appropriate thing to do**

4) The receptionist has likely come to Dr. Jess for a reason. She could have gone to Dr. Fillet herself. Also, Dr. Jess is better placed to speak to Dr. Fillet.**Inappropriate, but not awful**

5) Dr. Fillet is endangering his patients so this is an appropri-

ate action. However he should also inform Dr. Fillet of his actions.**Appropriate, but not ideal**

32. A 14 year old girl comes to the GP to ask for contraception. She says she would like to start a sexual relationship with a 15 year old boy. How appropriate are each of the following responses.

1) The GP must first decide whether the girl is competent to make decisions, and make sure that she has not been subject to abuse etc.**A very inappropriate thing to do**

2) This is not appropriate as the GP must first establish if there has been any abuse etc. There is also a right to confidentiality.**A very inappropriate thing to do**

3) This is not appropriate as the GP must respect the girl's right to confidentiality.**A very inappropriate thing to do**

4) This is appropriate, as the GP should act in the patients best interests.**A very appropriate thing to do**

5) This is not appropriate as the boy has a right to confidentiality, and does not help the patient.**A very inappropriate thing to do**

33. A patient who speaks very little English is about to be told that he is suffering from cancer by his doctor. He will need immediate treatment. How appropriate are each of the following responses.

1) There may be a misunderstanding. It is important to have a professional translator present.**A very inappropriate thing to do**

2) This would overcome the language barrier, but patient may not wish their relative/friend to know about his condition.**Inappropriate, but not awful**

3) This is a good course of action as it ensures that the patient will understand the information he receives.**A very appropriate thing to do**

4) This is a good course of action as it ensures the patient gets the information immediately and will understand it fully.**A very appropriate thing to do**

5) It is important to have a trained translator present to give the information.**Inappropriate, but not awful**

34. A 9 year old child has suffered a car accident, and is only able to breathe with a ventilator. He is fully paralysed, apart from being able to make eye movements, and there are no further treatment options available. The doctor in charge of his care has to decide what to do. How appropriate are each of the following responses.

1) The doctor should consult the child's family first.**A very inappropriate thing to do**

2) The doctor should consult the child's family first.**A very**

inappropriate thing to do

3) This is important as they should be involved in any decision.**A very appropriate thing to do**

4) His colleagues may be able to give ethical and legal guidance.**A very appropriate thing to do**

5) This is acceptable, however does not solve the issue of the decision that needs to be made, and he has not consulted the patient's family.**Inappropriate, but not awful**

35. A patient arrives in A&E. He immediately becomes angry and aggressive, and demands to be seen. A nurse asks him to calm down, at which point he begins to swear loudly. How appropriate are each of the following responses.

1) This may further antagonise the patient and could result in danger.**A very inappropriate thing to do**

2) This is very appropriate as it protects her and other patients. **A very appropriate thing to do**

3) This would help ensure her safety and that of the patient's, however they may take a while to arrive – she is better off calling the hospital security.**Appropriate, but not ideal**

4) The patient should not be given priority, however if she feels this will safeguard the A&E room, this may be acceptable.**Inappropriate, but not awful**

5) This is not appropriate at all as it could be construed as violence.**A very inappropriate thing to do**

36. A doctor wishes to talk to a competent 15 year old about a particularly sensitive issue. He has come to the practice with his mother. The doctor feels that the child may be discouraged the child from being open. How appropriate are each of the following responses.

1) The doctor should try and explain the reason why to the parent. He many also be wrong.**Appropriate, but not ideal**

2) This is appropriate as it means the mother can understand the reason why. The patient is then able to talk openly.**A very appropriate thing to do**

3) This would not be acting in the patient's best interests, however he is still a minor, and as such the parent has a right to stay in the room.**Inappropriate, but not awful**

4) This means he can find out if the child is able to talk openly with his mother present.**Appropriate, but not ideal**

5) This would mean that the patient is unable to see him in the present, which is detrimental to his health.**Inappropriate, but not awful**

37. A patient is coming to the end of their life, but lacks the capacity to make decisions on any further treatment. Time is of the essence. How appropriate are each of the following responses.

1) His next of kin would be able to make the decisions on his behalf.**A very appropriate thing to do**

2) As long as the doctor acts in the patients best interests, this is fine as the decisions need to be made urgently. However he should also try and contact relatives.**Appropriate, but not ideal**

3) This is appropriate as it may inform any decision that needs to be made. However this may take a while.**Appropriate, but not ideal**

4) This is very appropriate, as his next of kin is able to make a decision on the patient's behalf.**A very appropriate thing to do**

5) This would allow him to gain legal and ethical advice.**A very appropriate thing to do**

38. A patient wishes to access a certain treatment, however the doctor does not believe it is the right treatment. After further discussion, and full explanation of all the options, the patient's view does not change. How appropriate are each of the following responses.

1) The doctor is within his rights to refuse to treat the patient, but should also offer the patient the chance of a second opinion and/or legal advice.**Inappropriate, but not awful**

2) This is the most appropriate thing to do, as the patient can then choose which course of action to take.**A very appropriate thing to do**

3) The doctor is within his rights to refuse to treat the patient as long as he offers other options.**A very inappropriate thing to do**

4) This would allow the patient a second opinion, however does not solve the issue at hand.**Appropriate, but not ideal**

5) This is not appropriate as the patient may not wish to tell his/her family**A very inappropriate thing to do**

39. A clinician in an important research trial for an anticancer drug has discovered the possibility of a seriously harmful side effect unknown up until this point. How appropriate are each of the following responses.

1) The welfare of the triallists is of utmost importance.**A very appropriate thing to do**

2) This could result in serious harm, so is not appropriate.**A very inappropriate thing to do**

3) The clinician should also halt the trial.**Appropriate, but not ideal**

4) The clinician should first halt the trial.**Appropriate, but not ideal**

5) The welfare of the triallists is of utmost importance, so this is not appropriate.**A very inappropriate thing to do**

40. A doctor's son has come in to A&E after an accident. How appropriate are each of the following responses.

1) His son should be treated, however there is a conflict of interest, so should be treated by a different doctor.**Inappropriate, but not awful**

2) This is very appropriate, as there would be a conflict of interest if the doctor were to treat a family member.**A very appropriate thing to do**

3) His son should be treated no differently to any other patient.**A very inappropriate thing to do**

4) His son should be treated no differently to any other patient.**A very inappropriate thing to do**

5) This is acceptable, however simple acknowledgement would not take up any time.**Appropriate, but not ideal**

41. A doctor is examining a patient with a head injury when the patient racially abuses her. The patient then complains that she is hurting him, and refuses to be treated by her. How appropriate are each of the following responses.

1) The doctor should act in the patient's best interests at all times.**A very inappropriate thing to do**

2) This is the best course of action, as the doctor should act in the patient's best interests.**A very appropriate thing to do**

3) This allows for local resolution for the issue.**A very appropriate thing to do**

4) This is important, so the patient knows the doctor is not doing anything to harm him despite his behaviour.**A very appropriate thing to do**

5) This is an acceptable response, however the doctor should try to resolve the situation locally if possible. There may be mitigating circumstances (the head injury).**Appropriate, but not ideal**

42. A patient comes in to the general practice and gives his doctor a gold watch worth around £500. How appropriate are each of the following responses.

1) The doctor should consider his professional boundaries and the fact that the patient may have an ulterior motive. **A very inappropriate thing to do**

2) Regardless of whether he wears it or not, the doctor should consider his professional boundaries and the fact that the patient may have an ulterior motive. **A very inap-**

propriate thing to do

3) This is the most appropriate thing to do as the doctor has a professional rather than personal relationship with the patient. **A very appropriate thing to do**

4) This is a good thing to do, as the patient is able to understand why the doctor is not accepting the gift. **A very appropriate thing to do**

5) The GMC can advise the doctor on the best course of action**Appropriate, but not ideal**

43. A father comes in to the practice asking to see his 9 year old son's medical records. He is divorced from the child's mother (and does not have custody), and says that she refuses to tell him about the child's health. How appropriate are each of the following responses.

1) The father has a right to see his son's medical records**A very inappropriate thing to do**

2) This would allow the possibility of a resolution of the situation locally. **A very appropriate thing to do**

3) There may be references to the mother in the child's medical records, and the doctor must respect her confidentiality as well. **A very inappropriate thing to do**

4) This is appropriate as it protects the mother's confidentiality whilst allowing the father to access his son's medical records to which he has a right. **A very appropriate thing to do**

5) This potentially breaks confidentiality with the father. **Inappropriate, but not awful**

44. A nurse sees a patient in a bar 6 months after she helped treat him in hospital. The patient recognises her, and strikes up a conversation. They exchange numbers, and the patient later asks her out on a date. How appropriate are each of the following responses.

1) The nurse still may be inadvertently abusing the power of her relationship with the man. **Inappropriate, but not awful**

2) It would not be appropriate to start a relationship, however accepting the date may still lead the patient on**Appropriate, but not ideal**

3) It is inappropriate to start a relationship with an ex-patient, regardless of the time length**A very appropriate thing to do**

4) Her colleague would be able to provide some advice**Appropriate, but not ideal**

5) The GMC publishes guidelines on issues which the nurse can follow. **A very appropriate thing to do**

6)

162

45. A patient whose normal medication has been withdrawn from the market comes in to the GP to discuss a replacement. He has researched a new drug that is licensed in the US that he believes will suit him best. The doctor suggests a different drug based on the clinical guidelines; however the patient says that he tried this drug before and it wasn't as effective as the current one. How appropriate are each of the following responses.

1) The doctor should come to an agreed solution with the patient **A very inappropriate thing to do**

2) This keeps the patient on medication whilst the doctor is able to determine whether the other drug is useful **A very appropriate thing to do**

3) The doctor should not prescribe a medication to which he does not know or about, or which he does not feel will help the patient **A very inappropriate thing to do**

4) The doctor should not allow the patient to use a drug if he does not know anything about it, however he should make an effort to research the drug **Inappropriate, but not awful**

5) This allows the patient to express his views and feel listened to. **A very appropriate thing to do**

46. A 7 year old girl has been diagnosed with cancer, and is undergoing treatment. She has not yet been told of the nature of her illness (and has not asked). The parents ask the doctors not tell their daughter as they think it will cause her great distress.

1) The doctor should first establish the girl's ability to understand and handle the information as she is a young child. **A very inappropriate thing to do**

2) The parents have the right to make a decision as the girl is still a young child. She has also not expressed interest in knowing. **Appropriate, but not ideal**

3) This is a good plan as if the daughter does not have the capacity then she should not be told. If she does, then further discussion can take place with the parents. **A very appropriate thing to do**

4) The doctor needs to be careful not to lead the patient in one direction or the other. **Appropriate, but not ideal**

5) The doctor should still involve the parents and come to an agreed decision. **Appropriate, but not ideal;**

47. A patient who suffered from an illness a few months ago phones in to ask her GP if she can prescribe her the same medication she used before. She says she has been fine since, but wants to have some by her in case the illness comes back while she goes on a long holiday. The medication in question is very addictive. How appropriate are each of the following responses.

1) This would allow the GP to make a proper assessment of the patient's needs **A very appropriate thing to do**

2) This GP should not prescribe medication that would not be of any use. **A very inappropriate thing to do**

3) The patient has been fine without medication, so at the least should come in to the practice for a proper consultation before any prescription is made. **Inappropriate, but not awful**

4) The GP should not prescribe unnecessary medication, however she should further explore the patient's concerns. **Appropriate, but not ideal**

5) The GP should first explore the patient's concerns. **Appropriate, but not ideal**

48. A patient wishes to have further plastic surgery after having some a year before, but does not want the private surgeon to inform her GP. The surgeon wishes to contact the GP to establish if there are any other risks that may be pertinent. The patient refuses, and says that she knows the risks and that as she is paying, the surgeon should go ahead. How appropriate are each of the following responses.

1) The surgeon should not continue If he believes the patient's health is at risk. **A very appropriate thing to do**

2) The surgeon should not continue if he believes the patient's health is at risk, however she has consented and says she understands the risks. **Inappropriate, but not awful**

3) The surgeon should explore this and see if there is a possible solution. **A very appropriate thing to do**

4) The surgeon should not break the patient's confidentiality and go behind her back. **A very inappropriate thing to do**

5) If the surgeon is sure the patient understands the risks, then this is acceptable, however he should not compromise her safety. **Appropriate, but not ideal**

49. A mother comes in to the practice with her 8 year old child. She says her child is being bullied at school due to a large mole on his cheek, and wants to get it removed. She is divorced, and the child's father has not yet been informed. How appropriate are each of the following responses.

1) The father has a right to be involved with his child's care **Inappropriate, but not awful**

2) The child should have a say in what he wants to do **A very appropriate thing to do**

3) The father has a right to be involved with his child's care **A very appropriate thing to do**

4) Health is bio-psycho-social, and there may be a social/psychological benefit. **A very inappropriate thing to do**

5) This would establish whether there is a less drastic option available. **A very appropriate thing to do**

50. A patient comes in with a mole which has recently begun to itch. The GP refers him to a dermatologist, who suggests they remove the mole so they can test it further. The dermatologist tells the patient that there may be some bleeding and he will need stitches. Upon hearing this, the patient tells the dermatologist that he doesn't want to know what it involves, and to just go ahead with treatment. How appropriate are each of the following responses.

1) The consent is not valid as the patient is not fully aware what will happen**A very inappropriate thing to do**

2) This is necessary as the consent is not valid without the patient being fully informed**A very appropriate thing to do**

3) The patient should be fully informed, however the doctor should acknowledge the patients concerns **Inappropriate, but not awful**

4) The doctor cannot book the procedure without valid consent, but he should explain this to the patient rather than just not booking the procedure. **Inappropriate, but not awful**

5) This would mean that the doctor has booked the procedure without proper consent. Also the GP may not be able to explain the risks as effectively. **Inappropriate, but not awful**

51. A patient with a severe learning disability comes in with her mother to the GP. She has been agitated recently, and her mother is worried that something may be seriously wrong. How appropriate are each of the following responses.

1) The mother has experience with her daughter, so her opinion is valuable**Appropriate, but not ideal**

2) The GP should not assume the patient is unable to communicate. **A very appropriate thing to do**

3) This is important as it would inform the GP how to continue. **A very appropriate thing to do**

4) The mental health nurse would be able to communicate with the patient effectively. **A very appropriate thing to do**

5) The mother is likely to be able to contribute to the consultation as she is the patient's primary carer. **Inappropriate, but not awful**

52. A 15 year old boy comes in to the GP wishing to see the doctor. It is against practice rules for children under 16 to be seen without their parent or guardian. However the boy refuses to leave and is clearly distressed. How appropriate are each of the following responses.

1) It is important that young people have equal access to healthcare **Appropriate, but not ideal**

2) It is important that young people have equal access to healthcare. A chaperone ensures that nothing inappropriate happens. **A very appropriate thing to do**

3) The practice rules should be followed, however young people should have equal access to healthcare. **Inappropriate, but not awful**

4) This would establish whether there is a way around the situation. **A very appropriate thing to do**

5) Young people should have equal access to healthcare. This would not be the case with this response, **A very inappropriate thing to do**

MOCK TEST

Highlight your obstacles to success, work on them.

Time allowed 120 minutes

Mock exam questions
Verbal Reasoning – 22 minutes

Stem 1

Below is an extract from a study review:

This review has sought to evaluate all existing research concerning health care professionals' perspectives regarding telehealth. Several common beliefs, namely "Quality of Patient Care", "Implementation and Resistance to Change", "Face to Face Interaction", "Healthcare Professional Benefits", and "Locality and Convenience" have emerged from the literature. The majority of these provoked mixed opinions, with HCPs often divided on the issue.

One notable omission is the issue of cost. Very few researchers asked about cost perceptions, and the two that did only asked about remuneration procedures. The response was that they were undeveloped and would remain as barriers to the utilisation of telehealth until resolved. This lack of discussion of overall cost implications can perhaps be explained be noting that this issue would be more concerning to managers or policy makers, and not one considered by HCPs.

In addition to simply elucidating these perceptions, this review has discussed the potential reasons why HCPs hold these views. A factor potentially explaining why HCPs hold these beliefs could be age. Several of the papers identified that an age difference could explain the disparity between beliefs regarding telehealth. Younger doctors (or those with less experience) were found to have more positive opinions than older ones (or those with more experience).

Future work could perhaps seek to ascertain more conclusively what underlying factors, be they demographical or otherwise, contribute to these perceptions.

A major limitation of this review is that the identification and appraisal of the literature may not have been as thorough as that of an experienced researcher. Secondly, only published literature was considered (see appendix). Similarly, due to resource constraints, only articles with readily available access were appraised, limiting the scope of the analysis.

Questions

1) There are 5 common beliefs.

    True   **False**   **Can't Tell**

2) HCP stands for health care professional.

    True   **False**   **Can't Tell**

3) HCPs seem to be less concerned about financials compared to policy makers.

    True   **False**   **Can't Tell**

4) The more experienced doctors should be listened to according to the author.

True   **False**   **Can't Tell**

5)The author believes that the differing perceptions between doctors need to be examined to determine why they exist.

      True   **False**   **Can't Tell**

6)The review is not very good due to its limitations.

      True   **False**   **Can't Tell**

7)Younger doctors were more positive about telehealth than older doctors because they had less experience.

      True   **False**   **Can't Tell**

8)Older doctors have less negative views on telehealth than younger doctors.

      True   **False**   **Can't Tell**

9)Telehealth costs too much.

      True   **False**   **Can't Tell**

1) Which is least likely to be true :
   a. Younger doctors have less experience
   b. The review could have been better in its analysis
   c. Policy makers are involved in the financials of medicine
   d. Older doctors tend to be against telehealth as they have more experience

Stem 2

Below is a list of phases used by a group in a study on patient comments.

The six phases of Thematic analysis that we used include:
Phase 1: Familiarising yourself with your data
    Patient comments were typed up electronically, and then re-read several times by each member to ensure thorough familiarisation with the content. Initial ideas for codes were generated (for example, the prevalence of negative comments on transport, positive comments in relation to the service provided etc.)and noted down persisting with an inductive approach.
Phase 2: Generating initial codes
    Once all members were familiar with the content, interesting features of the data were coded manually. A code is defined by Boyatzis (1998) as being "the most basic segment, or element, of the raw data or information that can be assessed in a meaningful way …" Codes were formed in relation to information prevalence as well as their relative importance; if comments written by at least two patients revealed a significant finding relating to our research question, these were applied to generate a code. Consideration was taken to keep codes brief while still retaining the full meaning intended by the data.
Phase 3: Searching for themes
    After fully coding the data set, the codes were collated into potential themes which at times involved the

occurrence of cognitive conflict within the group, demonstrating the flexibility of thematic analysis to yield rich, varied analyses of data. When conflicting ideas emerged, each member justified their views which were considered equally among the entire group. Themes were derived using a quantitative approach based on their prevalence, and were also included based on their importance and relevance of each code to our overall research question.

Phase 4: Reviewing themes

A thematic map was produced and potential themes identified in phase 3 were reviewed. Some themes were redefined and some codes reallocated, illustrating the iterative process involved.

Phase 5: Defining and naming themes

Ongoing analysis lead to the refinement of the thematic map and members debated among the optimal name of each theme. The final themes agreed upon were: evaluation of the service at NPSDU; efficiency of sponsored transport; facilities at NPSDU; and the quality of care provided by the staff. Care was taken to avoid pitfalls described by Braun and Clarke (2006) by ensuring to fully analyse the data rather than simply para-phrasing the content.

Phase 6: Producing the report

The final step entailed producing a report which included a carefully selected compelling set of examples from the patient comments and a finalised thematic map in order to convey a clear and analytical understanding of the data to our reader.

Questions

1) The six phases involve production, defining, generation, reviews, familiarising and searching.

    True   **False**   **Can't Tell**

2) There was one person in the team that wrote the report.

    True   **False**   **Can't Tell**

3) A code involves changing the information into numbers or single letters.

    True   **False**   **Can't Tell**

4) Codes were kept to a maximum of a few words.

    True   **False**   **Can't Tell**

5) Themes were put together to form ideas.

    True   **False**   **Can't Tell**

6) The work done in phases 2, 3 and 4 were revisited and occasionally changed.

    True   **False**   **Can't Tell**

7) There were 4 themes.

    True   **False**   **Can't Tell**

8) We can assume a report was produced.

9)We can infer that Braun and Clarke suggested that simple paraphrasing was not the right way to analyse.

True   False   Can't Tell

10)The final thematic map will be clear.

True   False   Can't Tell

Stem 3

Below is an extract from a recent study:

A vast amount of data was collected but due to resource constraints, principally time, the depth of our research and post-collection analysis were bounded. This provides opportunities for future research, further delving into the complex relationships affecting patient experience at satellite dialysis units.

The most obvious example of this would be to focus on another facet of patient experience, other than waiting times, as established by the NHS National Quality Board (NQB, 2011).

Apart from measuring a different aspect of patient experience, future research could investigate waiting times more comprehensively, either by increasing the quantity of data collected or by increasing the depth of analysis. The increased data collection would result in a higher likelihood of obtaining normal distributions, which we failed to collect; this would enable parametric tests to be run, which hold more statistical weight than the non-parametric tests we were restricted to.

Additionally, nurses could be interviewed or administered a questionnaire to gauge a multi-stakeholder perspective on patient experience within NPSDU. This would lead to a deeper understanding about how the identified factors relate to waiting times, and provide a strong qualitative basis to inform possible areas of improvements.

As well as nurses, future work could also involve carers or family members who transport the patient to and from the unit, or accompany the patient during their dialysis treatment. Questionnaires could be administered to find out what they think could be improved, as they are also affected by the way the unit is run.

This study focuses on service quality solely from a patient experience perspective; however, future work could explore the cost-effectiveness and economic feasibility of each of the recommendations to ensure that efficiency savings are maximised, working towards the NHS Nicholson challenge.

Furthermore, interventional studies should be carried out to test the applicability and 'real-time' benefits of each of the proposed recommendations. This will reveal whether the recommendation in question actually has the scope to reduce waiting times or improve patient satisfaction prior to a longer term commitment of financial and human resources.

Based on the limitations of the questionnaire, quantitative questionnaires with a five- or seven-point Likert scale could be used to more accurately gauge patient satisfaction. If multiple significant relationships are found with satisfaction, a multiple regression analysis could be carried out to elicit the contributory role each independent variable plays on the dependent variable, patient satisfaction.

Further work should involve the use of both sequential and hierarchical process maps at NPSDU to guarantee that all aspects of the process are captured, as advised by Colligan et al. (2010).

To test the validity of the results, this study should be repeated at another satellite dialysis unit based around the hub of Hammersmith hospital, to study the differences in patient experience when the hub unit is kept constant, as well as other satellite dialysis units around the country. Confirmation of results would aid generalisability of findings to other satellite dialysis units on a national scale.

Questions

1) The analysis in the study was restricted.
   True   **False**   **Can't Tell**

2) The NQB is studying other aspects of patient experience.
   True   **False**   **Can't Tell**

3) The author says that the statistical tests in this study were not accurate.
   True   **False**   **Can't Tell**

4) If nurses had been interviewed, all the stakeholders would have been included in the study.
   True   **False**   **Can't Tell**

5) If nurses and family members/carers had been interviewed, all the stakeholders would have been included in the study.
   True   **False**   **Can't Tell**

6) The study has given ideas on how to improve patient experience.
   True   **False**   **Can't Tell**

7) It is better to adopt a recommendation for a short period of time to see its effectiveness before committing.
   True   **False**   **Can't Tell**

8) The results of the study cannot be said to be valid until further studies have been conducted.
   True   **False**   **Can't Tell**

9) We can assume that the results are only applicable to satellite units.
   True   **False**   **Can't Tell**

10) When was this paper written?
a. 2010
b. 2011
c. 2012
d. Unknown

Stem 4

Below is an extract from a study's Findings:

This study evaluated the service at NPSDU by measuring waiting times and satisfaction, two components of patient experience. The rising provision of dialysis treatment at satellite dialysis units, coupled with a lack of existing literature exploring patient experience in this setting, makes the results of this study particularly valuable.

Factors found to significantly affect waiting times were: mobility, transport, shift of the day, mode of vascular access and the area of the unit where a patient is dialysed. These factors were not found to have an association with satisfaction with overall care, with the single exception of area of the unit. We were able to speculate why these relationships may exist; however due to the inability to negate confounding factors, resulting from the obligatory use of non-parametric tests, we were unable to draw conclusions with greater statistical power.

The generalisability of these findings is limited by the unique characteristics of NPSDU. However, in multiple cases such as AVF, transport, unit area and mobility, we were able to draw somewhat generalisable conclusions on their effects on waiting times.

In general, patients who completed the questionnaire expressed a high level of satisfaction with the care. This, along with the limited significant results in the final satisfaction model, reveals that the associations between these factors and patient satisfaction are complex in nature, providing scope for future research. Thematic analysis of patient comments received from the questionnaires revealed four recurrent themes which helped guide our speculative discussion.

Based on our findings, a number of recommendations have been suggested to help reduce waiting times due to these factors. Most of the proposed recommendations are generalisable to other satellite dialysis units, and therefore, have the potential to improve patient experience with haemodialysis in a wider setting. These revolve around smoothing demand, improving patient flow and encouraging the use of Tesio.

All in all, this paper fulfilled the function of providing a stepping stone into evaluating the additional dimensions of patient experience within satellite dialysis units.

Questions

1) The study was conducted to measure waiting times and satisfaction.
   True   **False**   **Can't Tell**

2) The study was conducted to evaluate waiting times and satisfaction.
   True   **False**   **Can't Tell**

3) Waiting time differences did not correlate with overall care satisfaction.
   True   **False**   **Can't Tell**

4) It may have been better to use parametric tests if this had been possible.
   True   **False**   **Can't Tell**

5) There will be recommendations on how to improve satisfaction at satellite dialysis units.

True   **False**   **Can't Tell**

6) The reason for the paper could be said to help explore different areas of patient experience.
True   **False**   **Can't Tell**

7) NPSDU stands for Northwick Park Satellite Dialysis Unit.
True   **False**   **Can't Tell**

8) Not much research has been done in this area.
True   **False**   **Can't Tell**

9) The paper can be used by other satellite dialysis units.
True   **False**   **Can't Tell**

10) There are three main recommendations, and one minor one.
True   **False**   **Can't Tell**

Quantitative reasoning – 23 minutes

1. Below is a table showing repair claims for various makes of phone.

Make	Requests per 1000	Average cost per claim (£)
Blueberry	66	33
myPhone	75	45
Mockia	24	40
Clamshell	31	41
JYV	11	26

1) Which make has the highestcost per 1000?

   a. Blueberry b. myPhone c. Mockia d. Clamshell e. JYV

2) Which make has the lowest requests per 1000?

   a. Blueberry b. myPhone c. Mockiad. Clamshell e. JYV

3) myPhone release a new phone, but the requests for repairs doubles. How many requests is this per 100 phones?

   a. 15 b. 150 c. 75 d. 7.5 e. 9

4) myPhone decide to include a compulsory insurance scheme in their phone charges. If they wish to break even on repair costs, how much should they charge per phone?

   a. Can't Tell b. £4.00 c. £4.50 d. £3.37 e. £3.38

5) Clamshell reduces the cost per claim by 20%. How much is the total cost of repair per 1000 now?

   a. £3276.80 b. £2540.20 c. £1,016.80 d. £820.20 e. Can't Tell

6) Mockia have an increase of 25% in the number of requests. How many more requests are there per 100?

   a. 0.6 b. 31 c. 0.3 d. 6 e. Can't Tell

7) What is the difference in costs of repair per 1000 between Blueberry and JYV?

   a. £720 b. £1,034 c. £1.03 d. £7,000 e. Can't Tell

8) What is the average cost per claim across all the makes?

   a. 48 b. 47 c. 34 d. 37 e. Can't Tell

9) What is the average number of claims across all the makes?

   a. 49 b. 46 c. 47 d. 48 e. Can't Tell

10) What is the range in cost per 1000 phones?

   a. £960 b. £3,375 c. £2,415 d. £2,231 e. Can't Tell

2. Below is a table showing exchange rates across various fictional currencies.

1) How many Puros would someone get for 250 Curlings

   a. 307.50 b. 250 c. 300 d. 207.50 e. 400

2) How many Rollers would someone get for 1000 Juans?

   a. Can't Tell b. 0.34 c. 7.2 d. 7.3 e. 0.35

3) What is the exchange rate from Jens to Kesos?

   a. 4,032 b. 0.182 c. 0.124 d. 8.06 e. Can't Tell

4) What is the exchange rate from Fillings to Coronas?

   a. 0.92 b. 1.11 c. 1.1 d. 0.91 e. Can't Tell

5) If someone changes 100 Curlings into Rollers, with a 5% commission charge, how many Rollers would they receive?

   a. 160 b. 168 c. 59.4 d. 152 e. Can't Tell

6) If someone changes 100 Curlings into Puros, and then half of those Puros into Kesos, how many Kesos would they receive if the commission was 4% on each transaction?

   a. 2,856.96 b. 5,713.92 c. 5,952 d. 3,224 e. Can't Tell

7) The rate changes so that you can get 10% more Jen for the same amount of Filling. How much extra Jen would someone get for 856 Fillings?

   a. Can't Tell b. 400 c. 4,000 d. 8 e. 80

8) Someone wants to swap 100 Curlings, 100 Rollers and 150 Puros into Skand. How much Skand should they receive if there is no commission?

   a. 27, 875 b. 27,880 c. 43,561 d. 27,876 e. Can't Tell

9) The rate changes so you can now get 100 Skand for the same amount of Corona. How many Skand would you receive from 649 Corona if there was no commission?

   a. 18 b. 18.2 c. 550 d. 5.5 e. Can't Tell

10) The rate changes so you can get 65 Keso for the same amount of Puro. How many Keso would you receive from 13.53 Puro if there was 5% commission?

   a. 752.63 b. 753 c. 79.95 d. 750.95 e. 679.25

3. 112 people were interviewed with the following results. 70 people followed a football team, 38 people regularly went to the gym and 11 people were vegetarian.

1) What percentage of people were not vegetarian?

   a. Can't Tell b. 11% c. 9.9% d. 10% e. 90%

2) What percentage of people followed a football team?

a. Can't Tell b. 37% c. 38% d. 63% e. 62%

3) How many people followed a football team and regularly went to the gym?

a.Can't Tell b. 38 c. 19 d. 24 e. 20

4) How many people regularly went to the gym and were vegetarian?

a. Can't Tell b. 11 c. 10 d. 5 e. 4

5) If 2 people fell into all three categories, how many people fell into only one category?

a. Can't Tell b. 107 c. 110 d. 108 e. 100

6) If 1 person fell into all three categories, how many people fell into only one category?

a. Can't Tell b.106 c. 107 d. 111 e. 110

Water treatment

Water treatment is essential in converting polluted water to provide drinking water. The current waterworks converts 100 litres of polluted water to 50 litres of drinking water per hour, using 50units of energy in the process. One unit of energy costs £25

4)

---

1) How much does it cost to convert 1,000 litres of polluted water?

a. £11,500   b. £12,000 c. £11,750 d. £12,500 e. £12,250

2) The demand from the city is 800litres of drinking water per hour. How many waterworks are needed to supply this demand?

a. 14 waterworks b. 10 waterworks c. 12 waterworks d. 18 waterworks e. 16 waterworks

3) One new design offers to convert the same amount of water but using only 40 units of energy, with an initial cost of £2,000,000 how long will it take before the company breaks even in terms of the current design? Give your answers in hours

a. 8000 hours b. 8250 hours c. 8125 hours d. 7875 hours e. 7500 hours

4) The cost of energy has gone up by 25%. What is the cost of one waterwork working at maximum capacity for one day?

   a. £36,000 b. £37,500 c. £32,000 d. £38,500 e. £37,250

5)

> **The garden**
>
> Andy is an avid gardener and he want to redesign his garden. He goes to the local plant retailer where a rose plant cost £5, a daffodil plant costs £4, a tomato plant costs £6 and an apple plant £15.

1) How would it cost for Andy to redesign his garden using 5 rose plants and 2 apple plants?

   a. £47.50 b. £55 c. £65 d. £52.50 e. £50

2) His wife disagrees, she wants to redesign it using 10 rose plants and 3 daffodil plants, what is percentage increase of this redesign compared to his budget of £40?

   a. 50% b. 45% c. 55% d. 58% e. 60%

3) The retailer sells 165 rose plants, 55 daffodil plants, 132 tomato plants and 22 apple plants. What is the ratio of the rose, daffodil and tomato plants sales compared to the apple plants?

   a. 15:5:12:2 b. 12:5:15:1 c. 17:12:2 d. 15:7:12 e. 20:9:12:3

4) The retailer is in a seasonal sale, which is 25% off everything in store, what is price to resign his garden using, 12 tomato plants, 7 rose plants and an apple plant?

   a. £87.50 b. £105 c. £92.50 d. £91.25 e. £90

6)

Car Journey
Jane owns a car, she is going from London to Dover today, which is 77miles. She has to catch a ferry to Calais at 10am and her car gives her 40miles per imperial gallon. We presume that 60miles are on the motorway where the speed limit is 70mph and 17miles is in the city where the speed limit is 30mph

1) What time does Jack have to leave her house to catch is ferry? Providing she sticks to the speed limit

    a. 9am   b. 8.30am   c. 8am   d. 9.15am   e. 8.45am

2) How many gallons of petrol will be used for the journey?

    a. 1 gallon   b. 1.5 gallon   c. 2.5 gallons   d. 3 gallons   e. 2 gallons

3) The price of petrol is £1.30 per litre, 1litre is = 0.22 imperial gallons, how much does the journey cost?

    a. £10   b. £10.75   c. £11.70   d. £11   e. £11.75

4) There is road works on 20miles of the motorway and she is limited to 30mph, what time does she have to leave his house to catch the ferry? Providing she sticks to the speed limit

    a. 9am   b. 8.16am   c. 8am   d. 8.06am   e. 7.45am

Abstract Reasoning – 14 minutes

Question 1

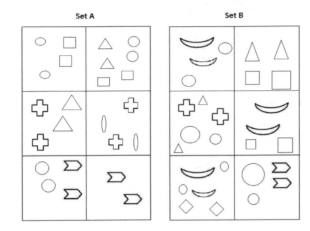

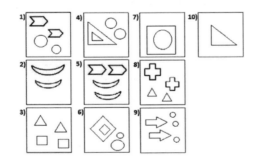

Question 2

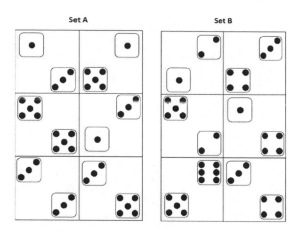

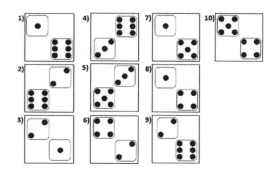

Question 3

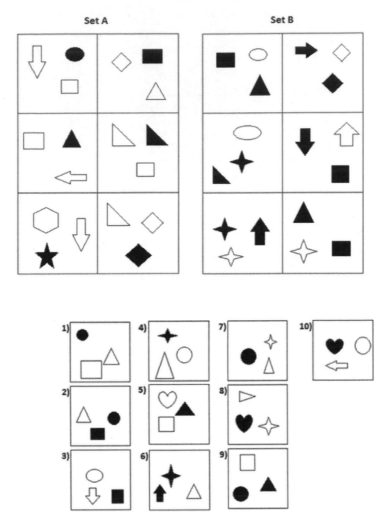

Set A

Set B

Question 4

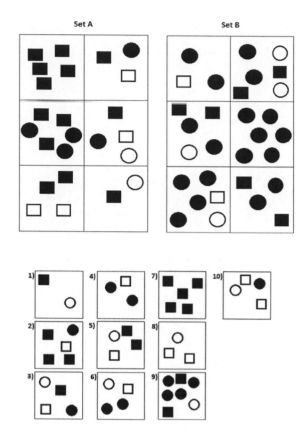

Question 5

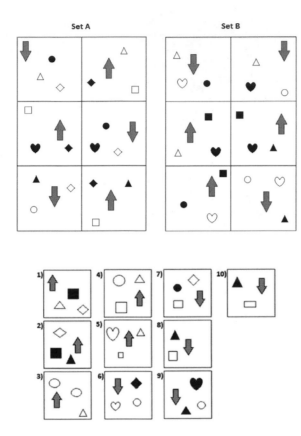

Question 6

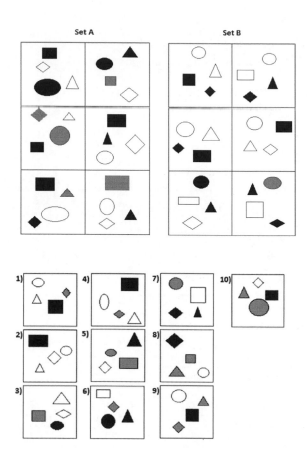

Question 7

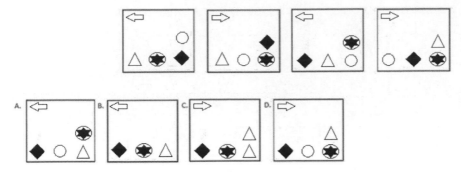

Question 8

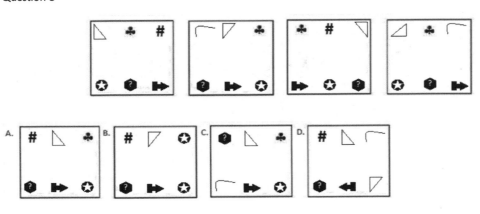

Question 9

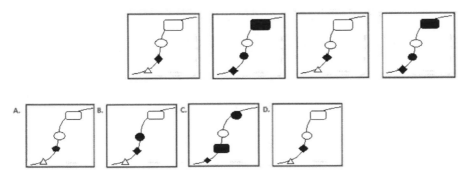

Question 10

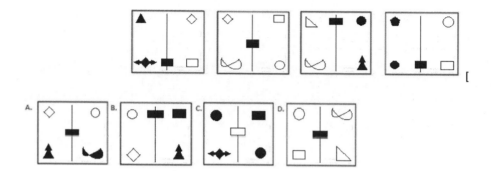

[

Decision Analysis – 34 minutes

Question 1

A = None	1 = Money	! = Large
B = Possess	2 = Gold	@ = Corrupt
C = Necessity	3 = Interest	£ = New
D = Many	4 = Bank	$ = Destroy
E = Opposite	5 = Save	% = Aggressive
F = Personal	6 = Loan	^ = Bad
G = Future	7 = Food	& = High
H = Combine	8 = Luxuries	
J = Allow	9 = Mortgage	
K = Away	10 = Government	
L = Present	11 = Building	
	12 = Official	
	13 = Recession	
	14 = Foreign	
	15 = Human	
	16 = Invest	

1) What is the best interpretation of the following coded message? @(D,12), B, 8

Corrupt officials possess many luxuries

The corrupt official possesses many luxuries

Corrupt officials have luxuries

Many officials possess luxuries

The official has many corrupt luxuries

2) What is the best interpretation of the following coded message? ^, H(6, 9), J, 13

Loans and mortgages are bad

The recession allowed people to have bad loans and mortgages

The recession allowed bad loans and mortgages

Bad loans and mortgages led to a recession

Bad loans and mortgages are recessive

3) What is the best interpretation of the following coded message? F, (5, 1), 4

The bank saves me money

I try to save money in the bank

I saved money in the bank

I keep my money in the bank

I save money in the bank

4) What is the best interpretation of the following coded message? (L, 13), (10, 16), %

During the recession, the government invests aggressively

The recession presented the government with an investment opportunity

The recession presented the government with an opportunity to invest

Governments invest aggressively during a recession

Aggressive government investment stopped the recession

5) What is the best interpretation of the following coded message? L, 7, (&,1)

Food is expensive

Food will be expensive

It is expensive to give food as present

Right now, food is expensive

Presents are more expensive than food

6) What is the best interpretation of the following coded message? L, (4, 6), (&,3)

Currently, bank loans have high interest rates

I am interested in taking out a bank loan

Bank loans will have high interest rates

Bank loans are very popular at the moment

Large loans from the bank have an interest rate

7) What is the best interpretation of the following coded message? 10, 11(E,G), (£,11)

The government are building new buildings

The government built a new building

The government will build a new building

The government will build new buildings

Governments build new buildings

8) What is the best interpretation of the following coded message? (L, 13), (14, 15), 16, (!,1), 2

During a recession, foreigners invest lots of money in gold

In the recession, foreign people invested large amounts of gold

Recessions allow foreigners to invest money in gold

Gold is a good place for foreigners to invest during a recession

Foreigners like to invest lots of money in gold during a recession

9) What would the best way to encode the following message be? Recessions destroy banks

13, $, 4

(13, $),(D,4)

(13, $), D

13, 4

(13, $), 4(D,^)

10) What would the best way to encode the following message be? Our government doesn't need any bad officials

(F,10), (A, C), 12(@, ^)

10, (A, C), 12(A, D)

(F,10), (A, C), (D,12)

10, (A, C), ^, (D,12)

(F,10), (A,C), ^(D,12)

11) What would the best way to encode the following message be? My family does not need luxuries

(F, 15), H(A, 8)

(F, 15), (C, 8)

F(D,15), (A, C), 8

(D,15), (A,C), 8

(F, 15), H(C, 8)

12) What would the best way to encode the following message be? New loans have a high interest rate

(D, 6), B, &,3

6, B, &, 3

£(D,6), B, &,3

(£,6), B, &,3

£(D,6), &, 3

13) What would the best way to encode the following message be? The government buildings will be destroyed

(10, 11), G, $

D(10, 11), G, $

(D, 11), G, $

D(10, 11), $

11, G, $

14) What would the best way to encode the following message be? The government has lots of gold

(B,10) , (!, 2)

10, B, (2, 5)

(D, 10), (!, 2)

10, (F,B), 2,

(B, 10), (2, 1)

15) What would the best way to encode the following message be? In a recession, people have less money

13, (D,15), (B,D), 1

13, 15, B, 1

13, (D,15), B(E,D), 1

13, (D,14), B(E,!), 1

13, D,14, B, E,D

16) What would the best way to encode the following message be? The government allowed the foreigner to invest

J, 14, 15, 16

10, (14, 15), 16

(10, J), 14, 16

(10, J), (14, 15), 16

J(14, 4), (10,16)

17) What would the best way to encode the following message be? The minister saved money in a foreign bank

^(10,12), (5, 4), (1, 14)

(10, 15), (5, 1), (14, 4)

(^, 10), 14, (5, 2), 4

(10, 12), (5, 1), (14, 4)

(10, 12), (5, 14), (6, 4)

18) Which two options would be the most useful additions to the codes in order to convey the following message accurately? The best food is often expensive

Most

Expensive

Time

Increase

Is

19) Which two options would be the most useful additions to the codes in the table above, in order to convey the following message accurately? He didn't need a mortgage to buy the building

Buy

Male

Need

No

Adult

Plural

Gives

Regime

20) Which two options would be the most useful additions to the codes in the table above, in order to convey the following message accurately? Gold is normally an expensive luxury

Single

Expensive

Generally

Normally

Often

23) Which two options would be the most useful additions to the codes in the table above, in order to convey the following message accurately? The prime-minister destroyed his opponent

Colleague

Beat

Enemy

His

Main

21) Which two options would be the most useful additions to the codes in the table above, in order to convey the following message accurately? My favourite food is cheap and light

Favourite

My

Light

Cheap

And

24) Which two options would be the most useful additions to the codes in the table above, in order to convey the following message accurately? My bank gave a loan to me during a crisis

A

My

Emergency

Give

Me

22) Which two options would be the most useful additions to the codes in the table above, in order to convey the following message accurately? The world bank offers regime's low interest loans

Low

Global

25) Which two options would be the most useful additions to the codes in the table above, in order to convey the following message accurately? Work on my house has begun

Start

My

Work

House

Past

26) Which two options would be the most useful additions to the codes in the table above, in order to convey the following message accurately? Corruption will not help my country

Aid

My

Public

Administration

State

Situational Judgment Test – 27 minutes

1. A woman comes into A&E with bruising. The triage nurse recognises her as she has been to A&E several times recently. She suspects domestic violence, and informs the doctor. The woman says she has fallen down the stairs. How appropriate are each of the following responses.

1) The doctor calls the police to report the abuse

A very appropriate thing to do

Appropriate, but not ideal

Inappropriate, but not awful

A very inappropriate thing to do

2) The doctor says that he does not believe the injury has resulted from a fall, and asks her if anything else has happened

A very appropriate thing to do

Appropriate, but not ideal

Inappropriate, but not awful

A very inappropriate thing to do

3) The doctor asks the patient to report the abuse

A very appropriate thing to do

Appropriate, but not ideal

Inappropriate, but not awful

A very inappropriate thing to do

4) The doctor does nothing as the patient says she has fallen down stairs

A very appropriate thing to do

Appropriate, but not Ideal

Inappropriate, but not awful

A very inappropriate thing to do

5) The doctor refuses to treat the patient until she admits what has really happened

A very appropriate thing to do

Appropriate, but not ideal

Inappropriate, but not awful

A very inappropriate thing to do

2. A doctor is in a consultation with a teenager in a psychiatric clinic. They have struck up a good rapport. The teenager asks the doctor if he is on Facebook, and whether he will accept her friend request. How important to take into account are the following considerations when deciding how to respond to the situation?

1) The vulnerability of the teenager

Very important

Important

Of minor importance

Not important at all

2) The doctor-patient relationship

Very important

Important

Of minor importance

Not important at all

3) The doctor's professional boundaries

Very important

Important

Of minor importance

Not important at all

4) The intentions of the teenager

Very important

Important

Of minor importance

Not important at all

5) How active he is on Facebook

Very important

Important

Of minor importance

Not important at all

3. A group of medical students have set up a group on Facebook that allows them to discuss patients that they have seen on their separate placements. A fellow student suggests that this may not be appropriate. How important to take into account are the following considerations when deciding how to respond to the situation?

1) The privacy level of the group to the wider public

Very important

Important

Of minor importance

Not important at all

2) The confidentiality of the patients

Very important

Important

Of minor importance

Not important at all

3) The scope for learning via this medium

Very important

Important

Of minor importance

Not important at all

4) The fact that Facebook is a social networking site

Very important

Important

Of minor importance

Not important at all

5) The fact that the fellow student is not yet a member of the group on Facebook

Very important

Important

Of minor importance

Not important at all

4. An elderly man comes in to the see his GP about his wife, who is also a patient at the practice. He is worried about some signs she has been exhibiting. A week or so later, the wife comes in having been in an accident that may have been caused by

some of the things that her husband had been worried about. The doctor pursues a line of enquiry based around this, at which point the wife asks if her husband has come in to talk about her to the doctor. How important to take into account are the following considerations when deciding how to respond to the situation?

1) The husband's confidentiality

Very important

Important

Of minor importance

Not important at all

2) The health of the wife

Very important

Important

Of minor importance

Not important at all

3) The likelihood that the husband is correct about the wife

Very important

Important

Of minor importance

Not important at all

4) Whether the wife and husband have a good relationship

Very important

Important

Of minor importance

Not important at all

5) A patient is suffering from a condition that impairs her ability to drive. The doctor has advised the patient that legally, he must inform the DVLA of the change in circumstances. However at the next appointment, the patient admits he is still driving and has not informed the DVLA. The doctor has to decide whether to inform the DVLA. How important to take into account are the following considerations when deciding how to respond to this situation?

1) The confidentiality of the patient

Very important

Important

Of minor importance

Not important at all

2) The safety of the patient

Very important

Important

Of minor importance

Not important at all

3) The safety of the public

Very important

Important

Of minor importance

Not important at all

4) The law

Very important

Important

Of minor importance

Not important at all

5) The severity of the condition

Very important

Important

Of minor importance

Not important at all

6. A patient suffering from a mental health disorder comes in to the GP after a recent stay in hospital to review his medication. During the consultation, a conversation develops around the issue of who would make decisions on his behalf if he was no longer able to. The patient decides that he wants to officially name his son as that person, even though his daughter is the one who looks after him. How important to take into account are the following considerations when deciding how to respond to the situation?

1) The view of the daughter

Very important

Important

Of minor importance

Not important at all

2) The view of the patient

Very important

Important

Of minor importance

Not important at all

3) The capacity of the patient currently to make such a decision

Very important

Important

Of minor importance

Not important at all

4) The doctor's own view

Very important

Important

Of minor importance

Not important at all

5) The likelihood that a situation will arise where this decision will come into action

Very important

Important

Of minor importance

Not important at all

7. Dr. Sellers, a senior doctor, is approached by a nurse who has been working with one of the trainee doctors on the ward. He complains to Dr. Sellers about the doctor's attitude on the ward, primarily to the nursing staff, as well as the patients. He says that the trainee doctor does not respect the nurses, and it causing problems within the team. How important to take into account are the following considerations when deciding how to respond to the situation?

1) The nurse's feelings

Very important

Important

Of minor importance

Not important at all

2) The view of the trainee doctor

Very important

Important

Of minor importance

Not important at all

3) Patient feedback

Very important

Important

Of minor importance

Not important at all

4) The availability of extra training in communication

Very important

Important

Of minor importance

Not important at all

5) The view of the university

Very important

Important

Of minor importance

Not important at all

8. A patient is being treated in A&E for a stab wound to his leg. The patient insists to the nurse that the stab was accidental, but the nurse does not believe him as there have been similar incidents reported recently. He informs the doctor, and suggests that the doctor contact the police due to the suspicious nature of the incidence. How important to take into account are the following considerations when deciding how to respond to the situation?

1) The safety of the public

Very important

Important

Of minor importance

Not important at all

2) The safety of the patient

Very important

Important

Of minor importance

Not important at all

3) The patient's opinion

Very important

Important

Of minor importance

Not important at all

4) The confidentiality of the patient

Very important

Important

Of minor importance

Not important at all

5) Where the patient was found after the incident

Very important

Important

Of minor importance

Not important at all

9. A patient comes in to see her doctor about a developing complaint. The doctor reviews her condition and suggests prescribing her a specific medication that is relatively new on the market. The patient is unsure, and asks the doctor what he would do in her position. How important to take into account are the following considerations when deciding how to respond to the situation?

1) The clinical guidelines

Very important

Important

Of minor importance

Not important at all

2) The doctor's own personal view

Very important

Important

Of minor importance

Not important at all

3) The doctor's professional view

Very important

Important

Of minor importance

Not important at all

4) The reasons for the patient's anxiety

Very important

Important

Of minor importance

Not important at all

5) The risk to the patient

Very important

Important

Of minor importance

Not important at all

10. A patient comes into the clinic for a regular check-up. Her doctor knows she has been subject to domestic abuse in the past, and finds out that her husband attacked her a few days ago. The doctor suggests that she contact the police, but the patient refuses. How important to take into account are the following considerations when deciding how to respond to the situation?

1) The safety of the patient

Very important

Important

Of minor importance

Not important at all

2) The confidentiality of the patient

Very important

Important

Of minor importance

Not important at all

3) The patient's opinion

Very important

Important

Of minor importance

Not important at all

4) The level of abuse

Very important

Important

Of minor importance

Not important at all

5) The likelihood the husband will attack her again

Very important

Important

Of minor importance

Not important at all

11. An elderly patient has been hospitalised with a serious complaint. The only treatment option available is surgery, which carries high risk. The doctors believe that it may not be in his interests to undergo surgery, and that they should discuss palliative care. The patient is unable to make the decision for himself, and his son and daughter disagree with how to proceed. How important to take into account are the following considerations when deciding how to respond to the situation?

1) Any previous indications of the patient on the issue (or similar issues)

Very important

Important

Of minor importance

Not important at all

2) Whether anyone has power of attorney

Very important

Important

Of minor importance

Not important at all

3) Who the patient's primary carer is

Very important

Important

Of minor importance

Not important at all

4) The amount of risk involved in the surgery

Very important

Important

Of minor importance

Not important at all

5) The views of the medical team

Very important

Important

Of minor importance

Not important at all

12. A junior doctor has come to see her senior consultant about some basic failings of care on the ward. He has noticed other people making several mistakes recently. Although there are no specific staff members at fault, the junior doctor is concerned that eventually one of these mistakes could lead to a severe incident. How important to take into account are the following considerations when deciding how to respond to the situation?

1) The timings of the mistakes

Very important

Important

Of minor importance

Not important at all

2) The type of mistakes –

Very important

Important

Of minor importance

Not important at all

3) Whether there are any specific personnel involved

Very important

Important

Of minor importance

Not important at all

4) Whether anyone else has noticed the mistakes

Very important

Important

Of minor importance

Not important at all

5) The competence of the junior doctor

Very important

Important

Of minor importance

Not important at all

13. A GP is in a consultation with a patient who has had a recent fall. The doctor is worried about the patient's ability to cope at home, as she has no support from friends or family. However the patient does not want to involve the social services as she wants to maintain her independence. How important to take into account are the following considerations when deciding how to respond to the situation?

1) The safety of the patient

Very important

Important

Of minor importance

Not important at all

2) The patient's personal preference

Very important

Important

Of minor importance

Not important at all

3) The level of intrusion that social services may inflict on the patient's life

Very important

Important

Of minor importance

Not important at all

4) The tasks that the patient will need to carry out at home

Very important

Important

Of minor importance

Not important at all

5) The patient's proximity to local amenities

Very important

Important

Of minor importance

Not important at all

14. Dr. Mellor has recently been diagnosed by epilepsy. Although there is treatment for the condition, he has admitted to having a brief seizure in the operating room that was missed by the rest of the staff. The doctor who is treating Dr. Mellor has to decide whether to inform the hospital of Dr. Mellors condition. How important to take into account are the following considerations when deciding how to respond to the situation?

1) The confidentiality of Dr. Mellor

Very important

Important

Of minor importance

Not important at all

2) The safety of the patient's where Dr. Mellor works

Very important

Important

Of minor importance

Not important at all

3) The severity of Dr. Mellor's condition

Very important

Important

Of minor importance

Not important at all

4) The fact that Dr. Mellor's condition is treatable

Very important

Important

Of minor importance

Not important at all

5) The type of work Dr. Mellor does

Very important

Important

Of minor importance

Not important at all

15. A patient with a terminal illness is admitted to hospital after attempted suicide. The attempt has left her severely brain damaged, and she is on a ventilator. The medical team have to decide whether to keep her on the ventilator. How important to take into account are the following considerations when deciding how to respond to the situation?

1) The ability of the patient to make a decision at this point

Very important

Important

Of minor importance

Not important at all

2) The fact that removing her from a ventilator may class as suicide or assisted suicide

Very important

Important

Of minor importance

Not important at all

3) The views of her next of kin

Very important

Important

Of minor importance

Not important at all

4) The patient's quality of life

Very important

Important

Of minor importance

Not important at all

5) The view of the medical team

Very important

Important

Of minor importance

Not important at all

16. Two patients require an organ transplant. One is aged 33, the other aged 60. The medical team have to decide who to give the organ to. How important to take into account are the following considerations when deciding how to respond to the situation?

1) The age of the patients

Very important

Important

Of minor importance

Not important at all

2) Which patient will gain the most from the treatment

Very important

Important

Of minor importance

Not important at all

3) The clinical need of each patient

Very important

Important

Of minor importance

Not important at all

4) The view of the hospital ethics board

Very important

Important

Of minor importance

Not important at all

5) The views of the patients families

Very important

Important

Of minor importance

Not important at all

Mock exam answers

Verbal reasoning

Stem 1

1) **True**. "Quality of Patient Care", "Implementation and Resistance to Change", "Face to Face Interaction", "Healthcare Professional Benefits", and "Locality and Convenience".
2) **Can't Tell**. The full wording for HCP is not given in the text.
3) **True**. The text says that the issue of cost is more concerning to policy makers.
4) **False**. The author does not give a personal opinion.
5) **True**. The author says that future work could seek to find out why the differences occur.
6) **Can't Tell**. There is no information on how 'good' the review is.
7) **Can't Tell**. This is not a conclusion that can be drawn. All that is said in the text is that the younger doctors have less experience.
8) **False**. They have more negative views.
9) **Can't Tell**. The text says that renumeration is undeveloped and therefore a barrier, but does not say it overall costs too much.
10) **Older doctors tend to be against telehealth as they have more experience.** The article does not say that – it says that older doctors are more experienced, and they have tend to be more negative about telehealth. There is no causal link identified.

Stem 2

1) **True**. These are a description of the 6 phases (although in a different order).
2) **False**. There are references to members (plural) and each member, so we know there was more than one person in the team.
3) **False**. A code has been defined in the text as something else.
4) **Can't Tell**. We do not know what the author means by 'brief'.
5) **True**. Themes were put together for analysis.
6) **False**. The work done in phase 3 was the primary area that was revisited.
7) **True**. Evaluation of the service at NPSDU, efficiency of sponsored transport, facilities at NPSDU, and the quality of care provided by the staff.
8) **False**. We do not know whether the rest of the report was completed.
9) **True**. We can infer this as the author says that they avoided pitfalls that Braun and Clarke described by not simply paraphrasing.
10) **Can't Tell**. We do not know if the finished version will be as intended.

Stem 3

1) **True**. The post-collection analysis was 'bounded'.
2) **Can't Tell**. The text suggests the NQB is involved in this area of research, but it is not clear what exactly they have (or are) studying.

3) **False**. The author says the statistical tests would provide better results if there were larger sample sizes. This does not mean the tests performed were not accurate.
4) **False**. The text talks about carers/family members who were not involved.
5) **Can't Tell**. We do not know which of the other stakeholders have/have not been involved.
6) **True**. Recommendations have been made.
7) **Can't Tell**. This is the authors suggestion, but we do not know this for fact.
8) **Can't Tell**. We do not know if the results are valid. The author says that the validity can be tested.
9) **False**. Satellite dialysis units.
10) **Unknown**. There is no date given.

Stem 4

1) **False**. The study was conducted to evaluate service.
2) **False**. The study was conducted to evaluate service.
3) **False**. One aspect (area of unit) had an association.
4) **True**. The author writes that they could not negate confounding factors as they had to use non-parametric tests. This implies that parametric tests would have solved this problem.
5) **Can't Tell**. The text only talks about recommendations for waiting times. We do not know about satisfaction.
6) **True** The last sentence says the paper fulfilled the function of providing a stepping stone into evaluating the additional dimensions of patient experience.
7) **Can't Tell**. There is no information in this text about what NPSDU stands for.
8) **True**. There is a lack of existing literature.
9) **True**. The author says some of the recommendations are generalisable to other units, so this is true.
10) **Can't Tell**. It's not stated in the text which of the three recommendations are major and which are minor.

Quantitative reasoning

QUESTION 1

1)Which make has the highestcost per 1000?

b. myPhone

myPhone costs £45 per claim (highest) and 75 requests (also highest)

2) Which make has the lowest requests per 1000?

c. Mockiad

Mockia has 24 requests per 1000, which is the lowest value in the table.

3) myPhone release a new phone, but the requests for repairs doubles. How many requests is this per 100 phones?

a. 15

Total new requests is 75 x 2 = 150. This is 15 per 100

4) myPhone decide to include a compulsory insurance scheme in their phone charges. If they wish to break even on repair costs, how much should they charge per phone?

e. £3.38

Total costs of repairs is 75 x £45 = £3,375 per 1000 phones. £3,375/1000 = £3.375, so £3.38

5) Clamshell reduces the cost per claim by 20%. How much is the total cost of repair per 1000 now?

c. £1,016.80

New cost per claim is £41 x 0.8 = £32.80. £32.80 x 31 = £1,016.80

6) Mockia have an increase of 25% in the number of requests. How many more requests are there per 100?

a. 0.6

Extra number of requests is 24 x 0.25 = 6 per 1000. This is 0.6 per 100.

7) What is the difference in costs of repair per 1000 between Blueberry and JYV?

b. £1,034

Cost for Blueberry is 66 x £33 = £2,178. Cost for JYV is 44 x £26 = £1,144. £2,178 - £1,144 = £1,034

8) What is the average cost per claim across all the makes?

d. 37

Total cost is 33 + 45 + 40 + 41 + 26 = £185. £185/5 = £37

9) What is the average number of claims across all the makes?

d. 48

Total number of claims is 66 + 75 + 24 + 31 + 44 = 240. 240/5 = 48

10) What is the range in cost per 1000 phones?

c. £2,415

Lowest cost per 1000 is by Mockia = 24 x £40 = £960. Highest cost per 1000 is by myPhone = 75 x £45 = £3,375. Difference is £2,415

QUESTION 2

1) How many Puros would someone get for 250 Curlings

a. 307.50

250 x 1.23 = 307.50

2) How many Rollers would someone get for 1000 Juans?

e. 0.35

1000/4509 = 0.221...x 1.6 = 0.35

3) What is the exchange rate from Jens to Kesos?

c. 0.124

Kesos/Jens = 62/500 = 0.124

4) What is the exchange rate from Fillings to Coronas?

c. 1.1

Coronas/Fillings = 118/107 = 1.10

5) If someone changes 100 Curlings into Rollers, with a 5% commission charge, how many Rollers would they receive?

d. 152

Curlings to Rollers is 100 x 1.6 = 160. Minus 5% commission is 160 x 0.95 = 152

6) If someone changes 100 Curlings into Puros, and then half of those Puros into Kesos, how many Kesos would they receive if the commission was 4% on each transaction?

a. 2,856.96

Curlings into Puros, including commission is 100 x 1.23 x 0.96 = 118.08. Half of this into Kesos is 59.04/1.23 x 62 x 0.96 = 2,856.96.

7) The rate changes so that you can get 10% more Jen for the same amount of Filling. How much extra Jen would someone get for 856 Fillings?

b. 400

Before, 856 Fillings would give 856/107 x 500 = 4,000. 10% of this is 400.

8) Someone wants to swap 100 Curlings, 100 Rollers and 150 Puros into Skand. How much Skand should they receive if there is no commission?

d. 27,876

100 Curlings is 100 x 98 = 9,800 Skand. 100 Rollers is 100/1.6 x 98 = 6,125 Skand. 150 Puros is 150/1.23 x 98 = 11,951. Total is 27,876

9) The rate changes so you can now get 100 Skand for the same amount of Corona. How many Skand would you receive from 649 Corona if there was no commission?

c. 550

100Sk to 118Co. 649/118 = 5.5 x 100 = 550Sk

10) The rate changes so you can get 65 Keso for the same amount of Puro. How many Keso would you receive from 13.53 Puro if there was 5% commission?

e. 679.25

65Ke to 1.23Pu. 13.53/1.23 = 11 x 65 = 715Ke. Minus 5% commission is 715 x 0.95 = 679.25

QUESTION 3

1) What percentage of people were not vegetarian?

   e. 90%

   112 – 11 = 101 not vegetarian. 101/112 = 0.901 x 100 = 90.1%

2) What percentage of people followed a football team?

   d. 63%

   70/112 = 0.625 x 100 = 62.5%

3) How many people followed a football team and regularly went to the gym?

   a.Can't Tell

   We have no information on the overlap between the two answers

4) How many people regularly went to the gym and were vegetarian?

   a. Can't Tell

   We have no information on the overlap between the two answers

5) If 2 people fell into all three categories, how many people fell into only one category?

   b. 107

   (70+38+11) – 112 = 7 'extra people'. 7 – 4 = 3 (subtract 4 for people in all 3 categories who have all been counted twice extra) 3 is the amount of extra people that don't fall into all three categories (two categories). 3 + 2 = 5 (total amount of people who fall into two or three categories). 112 – 5 = 107

6) If 1 person fell into all three categories, how many people fell into only one category?

   b.106

   (70+38+11) – 112 = 7 'extra people'. 7 – 2 = 5 (subtract 2 for people in all 3 categories who have all been counted twice extra) 6 is the amount of extra people that don't fall into all three categories (two categories). 5 + 1 = 6 (those who fall into two or three categories). 112 – 6 = 106

Question 4

1) How much does it cost to convert 1,000 litres of polluted water? **d. £12,500**

   - 1,000 litres ÷ 100 litres per hour = 10hours

   - 10 hours x 50units = 500 units

   - 500 units x £25 = £12,500

   - The demand from the city is 800 litres of drinking water per hour. How many waterworks are needed to supply this demand? **e. 16 waterworks**

   - 800 litres ÷ 50 litres = 16

   - 16 waterworks

2) One new design offers to convert the same amount of water but using only 40 units of energy, with an initial cost of £2,000,000 how long will it take before the company breaks even in terms of the current design? Give your answers in hours **a. 8000 hours**

   - Difference in the two designs = 10 units, 10 x £25 = £250 per hour

   - £2,000,000 ÷ £250 per hour = 8000 hours

3) The cost of energy has gone up by 25%. What is the cost of one waterwork working at maximum capacity for one day? **b. £37,500**

   - New cost of one energy unit, Increase in 25% = 1.25, £25 x 1.25 = £31.25

   - Total energy used in one day = 50 x 24 = 1200units

   - Cost = 1200 x £31.25 = £37,500

Question 5

1) How would it cost for Andy to redesign his garden using 5 rose plants and 2 apple plants? **b. £55**

   - 5 x £5 = £25

   - 2 x £15 = £30

   - Total = £55

2) His wife disagrees, she wants to redesign it using 10 rose plants and 3 daffodil plants, what is percentage increase of this redesign compared to his budget of £40? **c. 55%**

   - 10 x £5 = £50

   - 3 x £4 = £12

   - Total = £62

   - Percentage increase = difference in values/ the comparing value x 100

   - £62-£40/£40 = £22/£40 x 100 = 55%

3) The retailer sells 165 rose plants, 55 daffodil plants, 132 tomato plants and 22 apple plants. What is the ratio of the rose, daffodil and tomato plants sales compared to the apple plants? **a. 15:5:12:2**

- Rose:Daffodil:Tomato:Apple

- 165:55:132:22 all can be divided by 11

- Simplest form = 15:5:12:2

4) The retailer is in a seasonal sale, which is 25% off everything in store, what is price to redesign his garden using, 12 tomato plants, 7 rose plants and an apple plant? **d. £91.25**

- Original price = (12 x £6) + (7 x £5) + (1 x £15) = £122

- 1 = 100%, 25% off = 100%-25% = 75%, 75% = 0.75

- New price = £122 x 0.75 = £91.25

Question 6

1) What time does Jack have to leave her house to catch is ferry? Providing she sticks to the speed limit **b. 8.30am**

- 17miles ÷ 30mph = 0.566hours = 0.6 hours

- 60 miles ÷ 70mph = 0.857hours = 0.9 hours

- 0.9 + 0.6 = 1.5hours, 0.5 is a proportion of 60mintutes in a hour, the time is 0.5 x 60 = 30minutes = 1hour and 30minutes

- 10am – 1 hour and 30mintues = 8.30am

2) How many imperial gallons of petrol will be used for the journey? **e. 2 gallons**

- 77 miles ÷ 40 miles per gallon = 1.925 gallons = 2 gallons

3) The price of petrol is £1.30 per litre, 1litre is = 0.22 imperial gallons, how much does the journey cost? **c. £11.70**

- 77 ÷ 40 = 1.925 gallons = 2 gallons

- 2 ÷ 0.22 = 9.09 litres = 9 litres

- 9 x 1.30 = £11.70

4) There is road works on 20miles of the motorway and she is limited to 30mph, what time does she have to leave her house to catch the ferry? Providing she sticks to the speed limit **d. 8.06am**

- Total motorway miles = 60miles, 60miles – 20 limited miles = 40miles of unlimited miles.

- 17 miles ÷ 30mph = 0.566hours = 0.6 hours

- 40 miles ÷ 70mph = 0.571hours = 0.6 hours

- 20 miles ÷ 30mph = 0.666hours = 0.7 hours

- 0.6 + 0.6 + 0.7 = 1.9hours, 0.9 is a proportion of 60mintutes in a hour, the time is 0.9 x 60 = 54minutes

- Total time = 1hour 54 minutes, 10am - 1hour 54 minutes = 8.06am

Abstract reasoning

Question 1

Rule: In Set A, each matching pair of shapes is the same size. In Set B, one matching pair of shapes is of differing size, but the rest are of the same size.

Answers

1) Neither

2) B

3) A

4) B

5) A

6) Neither

7) Neither

8) B

9) Neither

10) Neither

Question 2

Rule: Set A has odd numbers on each die. Set B has one odd and one even number.

Answers

1) B

2) Neither

3) B

4) B

5) A

6) Neither

7) A

8) B

9) Neither

10) B

Question 3

Rule: Set A has one white shape with an odd number of sides, one white shape with an even number of sides, and one black shape. Set B has one black shape with an odd number of sides, one black shape with an even number of sides, and one white shape.

Answers

1) A

2) B

3) Neither

4) Neither

5) Neither

6) B

7) A

8) A

9) Neither

10) Neither

Question 4

Rule: Set A has an odd number of black quadrilaterals. Set B has an even number of black circles.

Answers

1) A

2) A

3) A

4) B

5) Neither

6) B

7) A

8) Neither

9) B

10) Neither

Question 5

Rule: In Set A, a circle means a downward facing arrow. No circle means the arrow faces upwards. In Set B, one black shape means a downward facing arrow. If more than one, the arrow faces upwards. Both sets have at least one shaded shape

Answers

1) A

2) B

3) Neither

4) Neither

5) Neither

6) A

7) A

8) B

9) A

10) B

Question 6

Rule: In Set A, the upper most shape is shaded. In Set B, the uppermost shape is a circle. There are always four different shapes.

Answers

1) B

2) A

3) Neither

4) A

5) A

6) Neither

7) B

8) A

9) B

10) Neither

Question 7

Box a.

What is consistent? There are the same five shapes consistently in each step, there is always an arrow in the top left corner.

Let's focus on step 1-2, the bottom four shapes in a L-configuration seams to move positions in an inconsistent manner. The arrow seams to rotate at 180º.

Does this pattern stay the same for step 2-3? Yes. We have identified the pattern, the rotation of the arrow at the top left and the same four shapes at the bottom.

Question 8

Box a.

What is consistent? There are the same seven shapes in the step they occupy the same space, along the top and bottom line.

Let's focus on step 1-2, The top three shape move in a left to right fashion, the club doesn't change, the right angle triangle seem to rotate 90° and the number sign seems to disappear, replaced by a curve shape. None of the bottom three shapes change however, they seem to move positions from right to left.

Let's see if step 2-3 follows are proposed pattern? Yes it does we have found the pattern.

Question 9

Box d.

What is consistent? There is a curve running from the bottom left corner to the top right, there are four symbols that lie on this line. There is constant unshaded circle in the middle of the curve, and there are a total of five shape shapes used in each step.

Let's focus on step 1-2, the rectangular looking shape seems to change shading but remains in the same position. In step 1, underneath the unshaded circle there seem to be a shaded diamond shape that moves down a position in step 2. The unshaded triangle disappears and a shaped circle appears where the shaded diamond was in step 1. The unshaded circle in the centre doesn't change.

Let's look at step 2-3, the shaded rectangle goes back to being unshaded like in step 1. We can make a pattern that it changes shade each step. Below the unshaded circle, the diamond shaded appears to change positions again, back to where it was in step 1. Along with this change in position of the shaded diamond the shaded circle disappears and the unshaded triangle appears again in the same position. Whether they appear or disappear must be dependent on the position of the shaded diamond.

Now we have made a pattern let's look at step 3-4 so see if it's correct. Yes it is.

Question 10

Box d.

What is consistent? There is a line in the middle with a shaded rectangle on it. The shaded rectangle seems to be moving in an upward motion on the line. There are shapes present on the four corners and these shapes appear to be random.

Let's focus on step 1-2, the shaped rectangle moves up, in step 1 the shapes to the left of the line are shaded and to the right of the line, unshaded. In step 2 the shaded rectangle is in the middle and there are no other shaded patterns. No obvious pattern yet.

Let's focus on step 2-3. The shaded rectangle is now at the top of the line, the shapes to the right of the line are shaded and to the left of the line unshaded. There is still no obvious pattern but we can start to suspect the position of the shaded rectangle box has something to do with the shading of the other shapes.

Let's have a look at step 3-4. The shaded rectangle starts again from the bottom, now, we can see the shading of the shapes, is exactly the same as step 1. The shapes on the left are shaded and the shapes on the right are unshaded. We have a pattern. The shading of the shapes split by the line depends on the position of the shaded rectangle.

Decision Analysis

Question 1

A = None	1 = Money	! = Large
B = Possess	2 = Gold	@ = Corrupt
C = Necessity	3 = Interest	£ = New
D = Many	4 = Bank	$ = Destroy
E = Opposite	5 = Save	% = Aggressive
F = Personal	6 = Loan	^ = Bad
G = Future	7 = Food	& = High
H = Combine	8 = Luxuries	
J = Allow	9 = Mortgage	
K = Away	10 = Government	
L = Present	11 = Building	
	12 = Official	
	13 = Recession	
	14 = Foreign	
	15 = Human	
	16 = Invest	

1) **Corrupt officials have luxuries**
   D means many, so it is corrupt officials (plural). The many is not linked with luxuries, and have is an acceptable alternative to possess.

2) **Bad loans and mortgages led to a recession**
   H(6, 9) means a combination of loans + mortgages, in other words loans and mortgages. J, 13 means allow recession, which means the same as led to recession.

3) **I save money in the bank**
   F Personal means I. There is no try or past tense in the coded message.

4) **During the recession, the government invested aggressively**
   (L, 13) literally means present, recession, which can mean during the recession.

5) **Right now, food is expensive**
   L means present, which can be converted to right now. (&,1) or high money can mean expensive.

6) **Currently, bank loans have high interest rates**
L means present, which can be converted to currently. There is no mention of interest, or popularity.

7) **The government built a new building**
(E ,G) means past, which when linked with building, means built. There is no plural in the code.

8) **During a recession, foreigners invest lots of money in gold**
L means present, which can be converted to during. Foreign human can be simplified to foreigner. Large money also means lots of money.

9) **(13, $), (D,4)** – (Recession + Destroy), (Many + Banks)

10) **(F,10), (A, C), ^(12, D)** – (Personal + Government), (None + Necessity), Bad(Officials + Many)

11) **F(D, 15), (A, C), 8** – Personal(Many + Human), (None + Necessity), Luxuries

12) **£(D, 6), B, &, 3** – New(Many + Loans), process, High, Interest

13) **D(10, 11), G, $** - Many(Government + Building), Future, Destroy

14) **(B, 10), (!, 2)** – (Government + Processes), (Large + Gold)

15) **13, (D, 15), B(E ,D), 1** – Recession, (Many + Human), Personal(Opposite + Many), Money

16) **(10, J), (14, 15), 16** – (Government + Allow), (Foreign + Human), Invest

17) **(10, 12), (5, 1), (14, 4)** –(Government + Official), (Save + Money), (Foreign + Bank)

18) **Most**
Time

Expensive can be coded for by large or high money. Increase is not necessary to help the convey the message. Is is not necessary for codes in general.

19) **Male**
Buy

Need can be coded for by necessity. No would not help convey the message. There is no mention of adult in the mention.

20) **Normally**
Single

Expensive can be coded for by large or high money. If we use normally, we do not need generally. If we use normally, we do not need often.

21) **Favourite**
Light

Personal can code for my. Cheap can be coded for by opposite large/high money. And is not necessary for codes in general.

22) **Global**
Gives

Low can be coded by opposite high. Many can be used instead of plural. Government is adequate for regime, as there are no replacements for global or gives.

23) **Main**
Enemy

Enemy is more accurate than colleague. Destroy is already a

code, so beat is not necessary. His can be coded for by personal - Main and enemy are more important to get the message across.

24) **Give**
Emergency

My and me can be coded for by personal. A is not necessary for codes in general.

25) **Work**
Start

My can be coded for using personal. House can be written as personal building. Past can be coded for by opposite future.

26) **State**
Aid

My can be coded for using personal. Public and administration are both not in the message.

Situational judgment tests

1. **A woman comes into A&E with bruising. The triage nurse recognises her as she has been to A&E several times recently. She suspects domestic violence, and informs the doctor. The woman says she has fallen down the stairs. How appropriate are each of the following responses.**

1) The doctor should try and get the information from the patient first **A very inappropriate thing to do**

2) This allows the patient to come forward and explain what has really happened **A very appropriate thing to do**

3) The doctor should not make assumptions, and should get the patient to explain what has happened first **Appropriate, but not ideal**;

4) If a different reason is suspected, especially one that puts the patient's safety at risk, the doctor should not just accept the reason **A very inappropriate thing to do**

5) The doctor should do what is in the patient's best interests, as well as doing the least harm **A very inappropriate thing to do**

2.A doctor is in a consultation with a teenager in a psychiatric clinic. They have struck up a good rapport. The teenager asks the doctor if he is on Facebook, and whether he will accept her friend request. How important to take into account are the following considerations when deciding how to respond to the situation?

1) This is extremely important as the doctor needs to be sensitive in however he responds. The doctor must respect professional boundaries. **Very important**

2) It is important to maintain the relationship as it is, as the patient needs to understand the role of the doctor. **Very important**

3) The doctor should be wary of getting close to the patient especially as she is vulnerable. **Very important**

4) If the teenager merely wishes to be friends on Facebook, a different response is needed to if she wishes to strike up a close relationship with the doctor. **Very important**

5) Regardless of how active he is on Facebook, the doctor should maintain certain boundaries. **Of minor importance**

3. A group of medical students have set up a group on Facebook that allows them to discuss patients that they have seen on their separate placements. A fellow student suggests that this may not be appropriate. How important to take into account are the following considerations when deciding how to respond to the situation?

1) If the group is private, the medical students may not be doing anything wrong. However with sites like Facebook, site administrators have access to a lot of material so the group may never be completely private.**Important**

2) Patient confidentiality should never be sacrificed for the sake of a learning opportunity. **Very important**

3) There are other ways to learn, so even if this is a particularly effective way to learn, other issues such as confidentiality are more important. **Of minor importance**

4) This does not play a factor in any decision. **Not important at all**

5) The student has a valid concern, so her reasons for speaking up are immaterial. **Not important at all**

4. An elderly man comes in to the see his GP about his wife, who is also a patient at the practice. He is worried about some signs she has been exhibiting. A week or so later, the wife comes in having been in an accident that may have been caused by some of the things that her husband had been worried about. The doctor pursues a line of enquiry based around this, at which point the wife asks if her husband has come in to talk about her to the doctor. How important to take into account are the following considerations when deciding how to respond to the situation?

1) The husband has come to see the GP in confidence. By breaking confidentiality, the GP loses his trust. **Very important**

2) The health of the wife is the main problem here, so this is of utmost importance. The GP should look to do the least harm. **Very important**

3) It does not matter whether he is right or wrong, just that he is worried. **Not important at all**

4) The GP should try not to deceive any patient, however there are ways to protect the husband's confidentiality as well as not lying to the wife. **Of minor importance**

5. A patient is suffering from a condition that impairs her ability to drive. The doctor has advised the patient that legally, he must

inform the DVLA of the change in circumstances. However at the next appointment, the patient admits he is still driving and has not informed the DVLA. The doctor has to decide whether to inform the DVLA. How important to take into account are the following considerations when deciding how to respond to this situation?

1) The GP should try to make sure the patient does not lose trust by respecting her confidentiality. However there are ways around this.**Important**

2) The patient's safety and health should be at the forefront of the GP's mind at all times.**Very important**

3) The safety of the public is just as important as the patient – by driving around she is risking other people's safety.**Very important**

4) The law is there for a reason, and the GP should respect this wherever possible. **Very important**

5) The fact that the condition impairs her ability to drive means that regardless of the severity, the DVLA should be informed. However, this could inform the urgency with which the GP should act.**Of minor importance**

6. A patient suffering from a mental health disorder comes in to the GP after a recent stay in hospital to review his medication. During the consultation, a conversation develops around the issue of who would make decisions on his behalf if he was no longer able to. The patient decides that he wants to officially name his son as that person, even though his daughter is the one who looks after him. How important to take into account are the following considerations when deciding how to respond to the situation?

1) The daughters view should be taken into account as she is the patient's primary carer. **Of minor importance**

2) As this decision is about the patient, the patient should have the ultimate decision, so his view is the most important. **Very important**

3) If the patient is currently not competent to make a decision, then any decision he does make cannot be accepted.**Very important**

4) The doctor should have no say as this is a personal/family issue rather than a health issue. **Not important at all**

5) The likelihood that the situation will arise does not matter. **Not important at all**

7. Dr. Sellers, a senior doctor, is approached by a nurse who has been working with one of the trainee doctors on the ward. He complains to Dr. Sellers about the doctor's attitude on the ward, primarily to the nursing staff, as well as the patients. He says that the trainee doctor does not respect the nurses, and it causing problems within the team. How important to take into account are the following considerations when deciding how to respond to the situation?

1) The nurse is well placed to observe the trainee. **Very important**

2) Dr. Sellers should not make any decisions without seeing what the trainee doctor thinks – he may disagree, which would suggest a different issue. **Very important**

3) The patients would be able to tell Dr. Sellers if they are happy with the standard of care they are receiving from the trainee. **Very important**

4) This would inform the decision of Dr. Sellers on what to do, assuming the trainee was in fact causing problems. However it is more important to establish the facts first. **Of minor importance**

5) The university should be informed, but as they are not involved directly with his training on the ward, their view should not matter.**Not important at all**

8. A patient is being treated in A&E for a stab wound to his leg. The patient insists to the nurse that the stab was accidental, but the nurse does not believe him as there have been similar incidents reported recently. He informs the doctor, and suggests that the doctor contact the police due to the suspicious nature of the incidence. How important to take into account are the following considerations when deciding how to respond to the situation?

1) The safety of the public is extremely important, and may trump the patient's confidentiality **Very important**

2) The safety and health of the patient should be at the forefront of the doctor's mind **Very important**

3) The patient should be involved with any decision made as it is him who will face the consequences **Very important**

4) The patient should not lose trust in the healthcare system. However the safety of the public may trump this.**Important**

5) This could help the doctor decide the likelihood that the stab wound is accidental.**Of minor importance**

9. A patient comes in to see her doctor about a developing complaint. The doctor reviews her condition and suggests prescribing her a specific medication that is relatively new on the market. The patient is unsure, and asks the doctor what he would do in her position. How important to take into account are the following considerations when deciding how to respond to the situation?

1) The clinical guidelines have been set up by experts who have weighed up the evidence. They should be followed where possible **Very important**

2) The doctor's personal view is not important as it is the patient who will be taking the medication **Not important at all**

3) The doctor's professional view is important as he will be able to inform the patient about risks/benefits **Important**

4) This could allow the doctor to reassure the patient **Very important**

5) The risk to the patient is very important, the doctor should look to do the least harm **Very important**

10. A patient comes into the clinic for a regular check-up. Her doctor knows she has been subject to domestic abuse in the past, and finds out that her husband attacked her a few days ago. The doctor suggests that she contact the police, but the patient refuses. How important to take into account are the following considerations when deciding how to respond to the situation?

1) The patient's health and safety should be at the forefront of the doctor's mind at all times **Very important**

2) The patient should be able to trust her doctor. However her safety may be of a higher importance. **Important**

3) This is the patient's life, so her opinion is the most important. **Very important**

4) The level of abuse may indicate whether the patient needs to stay in a refuge, and whether she requires protection etc.**Of minor importance**

5) The fact that the husband has attacked her is enough to warrant police involvement. However if the patient refuses, this is a factor to take into account**Of minor importance**

11. An elderly patient has been hospitalised with a serious complaint. The only treatment option available is surgery, which carries high risk. The doctors believe that it may not be in his interests to undergo surgery, and that they should discuss palliative care. The patient is unable to make the decision for himself, and his son and daughter disagree with how to proceed. How important to take into account are the following considerations when deciding how to respond to the situation?

1) As the patient's family cannot agree, any previous indications may give an insight into his wishes. **Important**

2) Whoever has power of attorney is able to make the decision **Very important**

3) The patient's primary carer may have a greater insight into the wishes of the patient, however all family members should have an equal say **Of minor importance**

4) This would inform the family and medical team whether surgery would be useful **Important**

5) The medical team would be able to give their professional views, however ultimately it is the family's decision **Of minor importance**

12. A junior doctor has come to see her senior consultant about some basic failings of care on the ward. He has noticed other people making several mistakes recently. Although there are no specific staff members at fault, the junior doctor is concerned that eventually one of these mistakes could lead to a severe incident. How important to take into account are the following considerations when deciding how to respond to the situation?

1) This could provide an indication of if there is a specific reason for the mistakes **Important**

2) The fact that there are mistakes is most important. The type could help the consultant decide what action needs to be taken – training, or simply awareness.**Of minor importance**

3) This would help the consultant decide what action to take – people may need further training. **Very important**

4) There is no reason to suggest the junior doctor is not telling the truth. However a second opinion may help the consultant isolate the incidents**Of minor importance**

5) This is not important as he has noticed other people making mistakes. **Not important at all**

13. A GP is in a consultation with a patient who has had a recent fall. The doctor is worried about the patient's ability to cope at home, as she has no support from friends or family. However the patient does not want to involve the social services as she wants to maintain her independence. How important to take into account are the following considerations when deciding how to respond to the situation?

1) The patient's health and safety should be at the forefront of the doctor's mind at all times **Very important**

2) As this is the patient's life, any involvement of social services should be her decision **Very important**

3) The patient should not be inconvenienced where possible. However her safety is also very important **Important**

4) This would help the doctor decide whether help is necessary. **Important**

5) This would help the doctor decide whether help is necessary **Important**

14. Dr. Mellor has recently been diagnosed by epilepsy. Although there is treatment for the condition, he has admitted to having a brief seizure in the operating room that was missed by the rest of the staff. The doctor who is treating Dr. Mellor has to decide whether to inform the hospital of Dr. Mellors condition. How important to take into account are the following considerations when deciding how to respond to the situation?

1) Dr. Mellor's confidentiality should be respected, however in this case the safety of the patient's where he works is more important **Of minor importance**

2) This is of utmost importance, especially due to where he works – his condition should not harm others **Very important**

3) The fact that he has had a seizure in the operating room means it could happen again **Of minor importance**

4) This should be mentioned to his employers, however the fact that he has had a seizure at work means it could happen again **Of minor importance**

5) This is very important as he is involved with lots of patients, each of whom could be in danger **Very important**

15. A patient with a terminal illness is admitted to hospital after attempted suicide. The attempt has left her severely brain damaged, and she is on a ventilator. The medical team have to decide whether to keep her on the ventilator. How important to take into account are the following considerations when deciding how to respond to the situation?

1) If she is not able to make a decision, her family should be informed (or whoever has power of attorney). **Very important**

2) The doctor's should not do anything illegal when deciding how to act. **Important**

3) If she is not able to make a decision, her decision should be passed on to next of kin. **Very important**

4) This is important as if she is going to have a severely reduced quality of life, then it may be better to take her off the ventilator. **Very important**

5) The medical team should give their professional advice to the family, but ultimately the decision rests with the family. **Of minor importance**

16. Two patients require an organ transplant. One is aged 33, the other aged 60. The medical team have to decide who to give the organ to. How important to take into account are the following considerations when deciding how to respond to the situation?

1) The age does not matter as the organ should go the person who needs it most. **Not important at all**

2) The organ should go to the person who needs it most. **Not important at all**

3) The clinical need is what should determine who receives the organ **Very important**

4) The hospital ethics board would be able to decide impartially who needs the organ the most **Very important**

5) The organ should go to the person who needs it most. So in this case, the patients family's would not have a say. **Not important at all**

Concluding remarks

- We strongly advise that you get a good night's sleep the day before your test. Being rested will ensure that you deliver your best on the day. Ensure that you leave in good time to account for any delays in travel, or any unforeseen incidents. This will enable you to arrive early at the test centre and just relax.

- If during the test, you get anxious or your mind goes blank, don't panic! Take a few seconds to breathe and get your thoughts together. Remind yourself that this is a perseverance test as well and now is not the time to give up.

- Old format questions are good; they use the same skills you need for the new format of questions. They will help you develop a good sense of understanding.

- Use real life as you your best resource

- Work on your weaknesses, improve yourself

We hope you make the most of this resource combined with others around you and wish you all the best with your UKCAT!

If you enjoyed the book please do leave us good feedback on amazon.

If you have any questions or queries with regards to this book, please feel free to email us at:

info@ukcatcourses.co.uk

Thank you for buying our book, and we wish you the best of luck in you exam.

6752951R00124

Printed in Great Britain
by Amazon.co.uk, Ltd.,
Marston Gate.